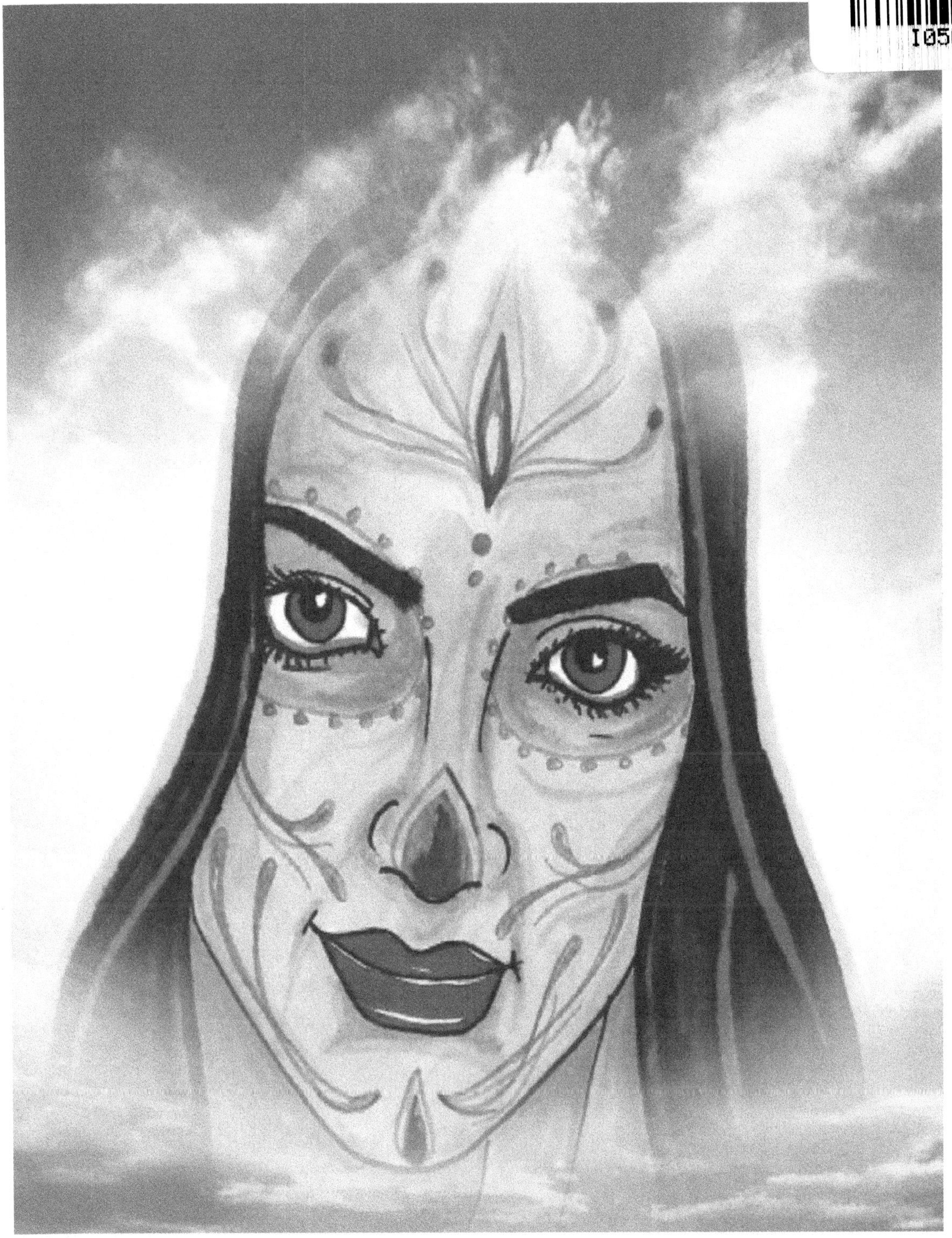

This Book Dedicated to my

Parents.

Fernando Sr, and Dioni

Let your Imagination

run free.

Nothing is wrong.

Do what you feel.

Enjoy!

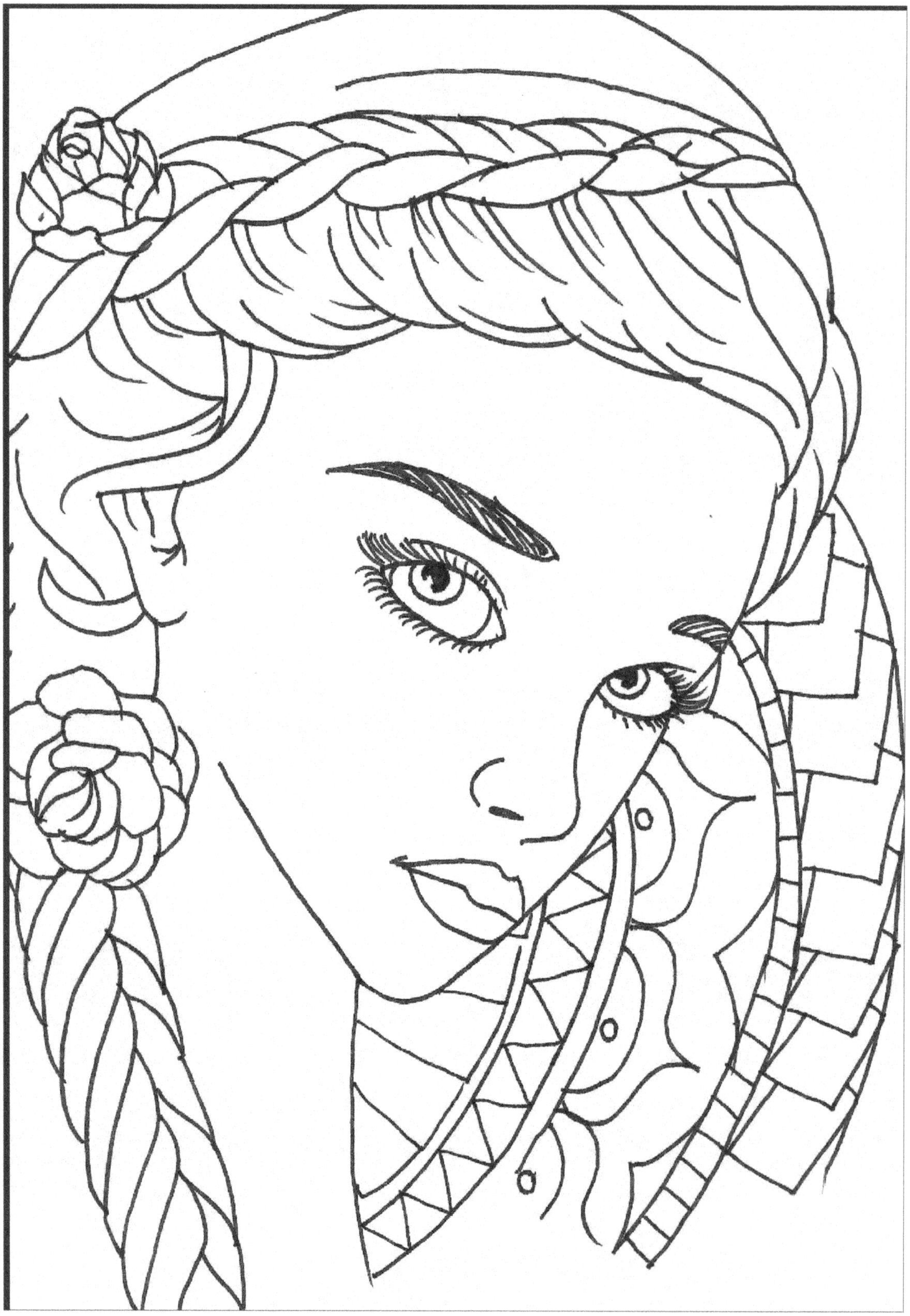

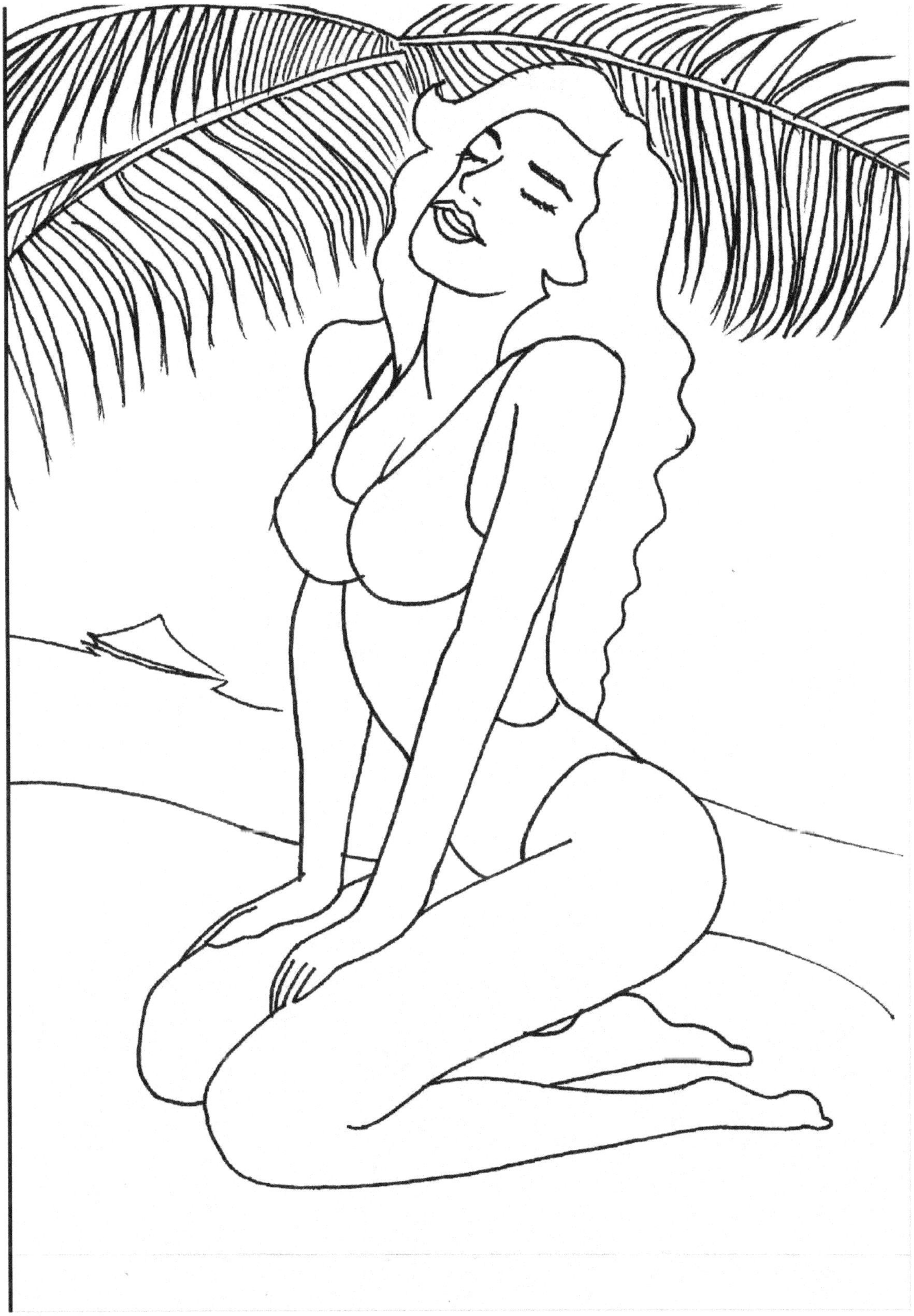

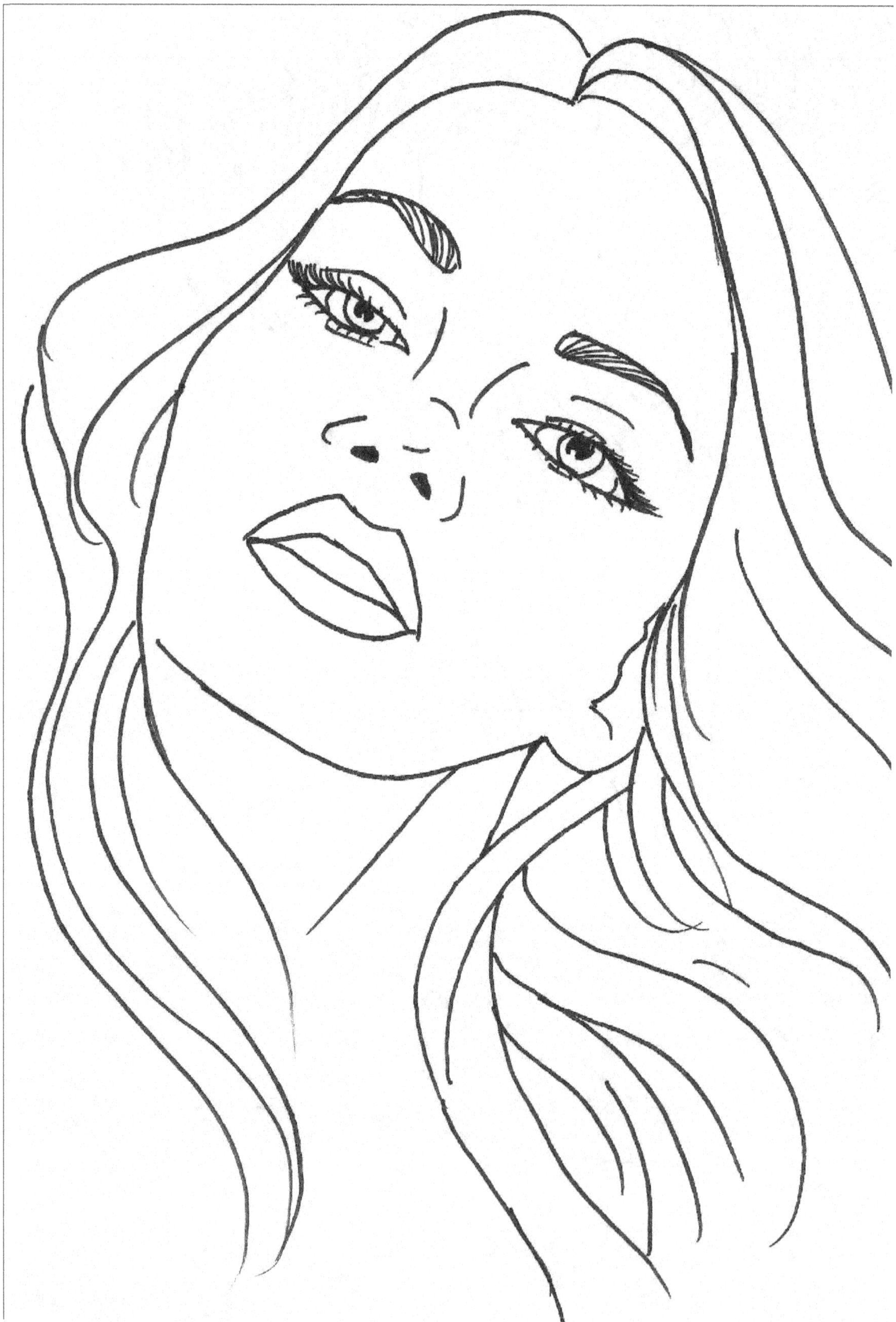

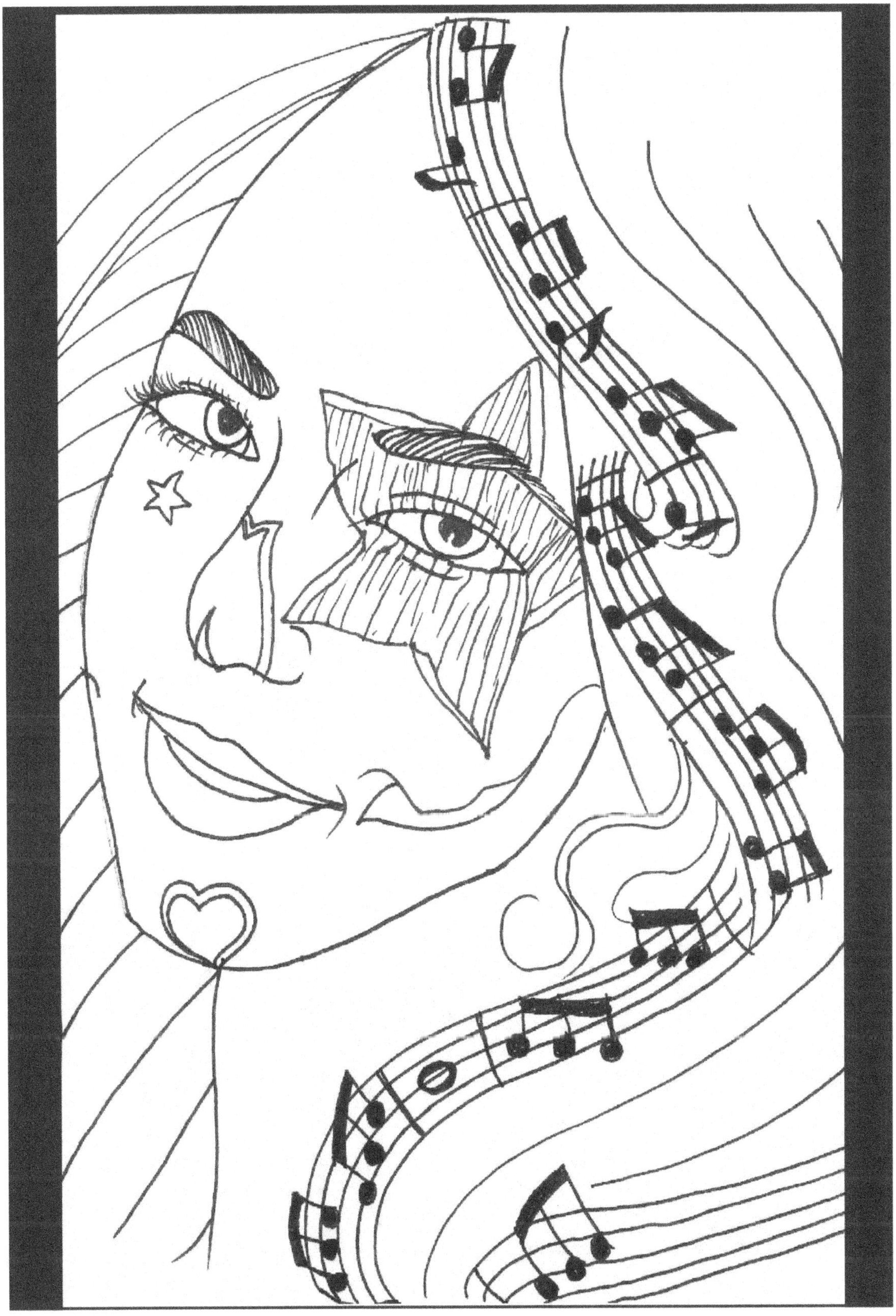

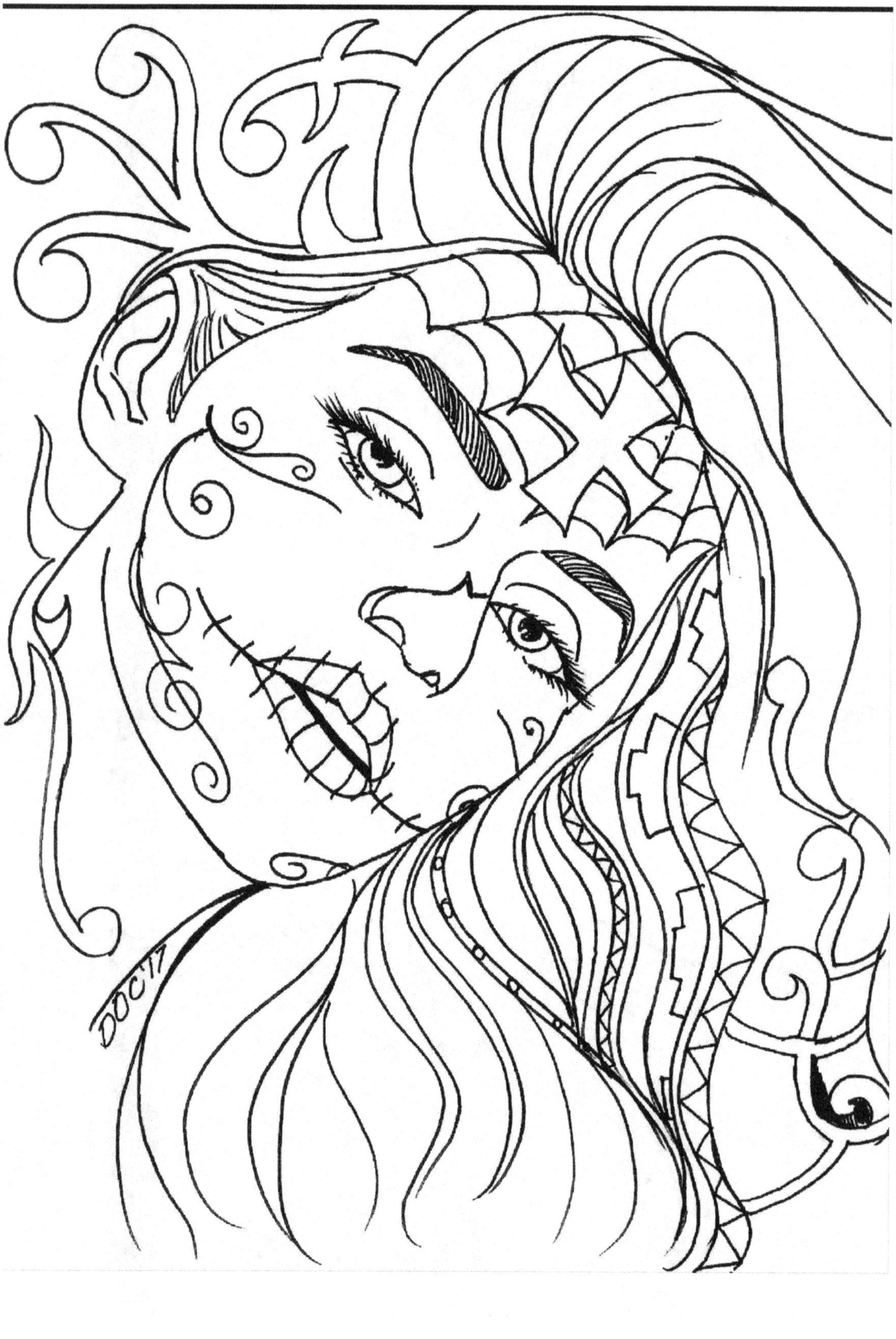
DOC'17

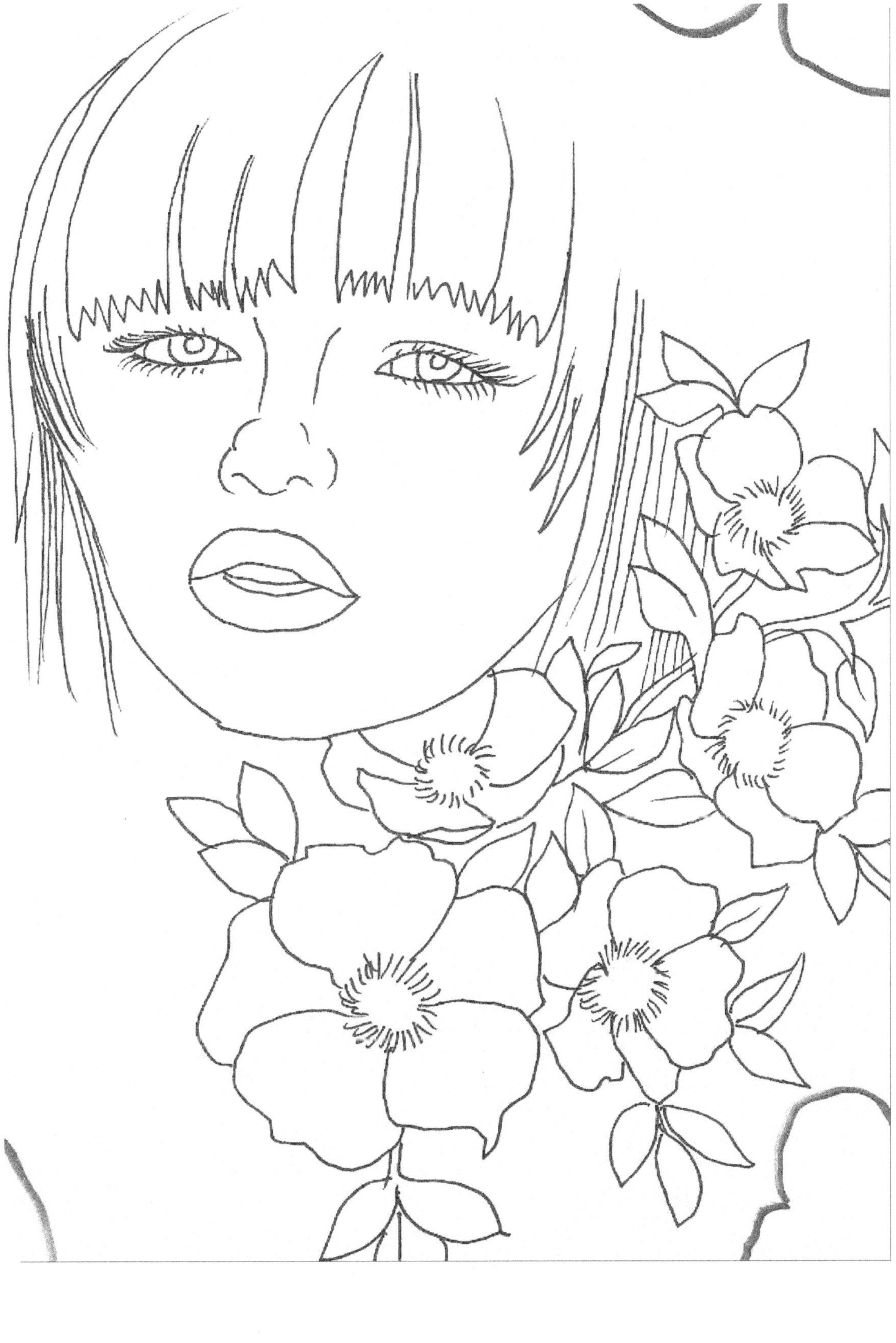

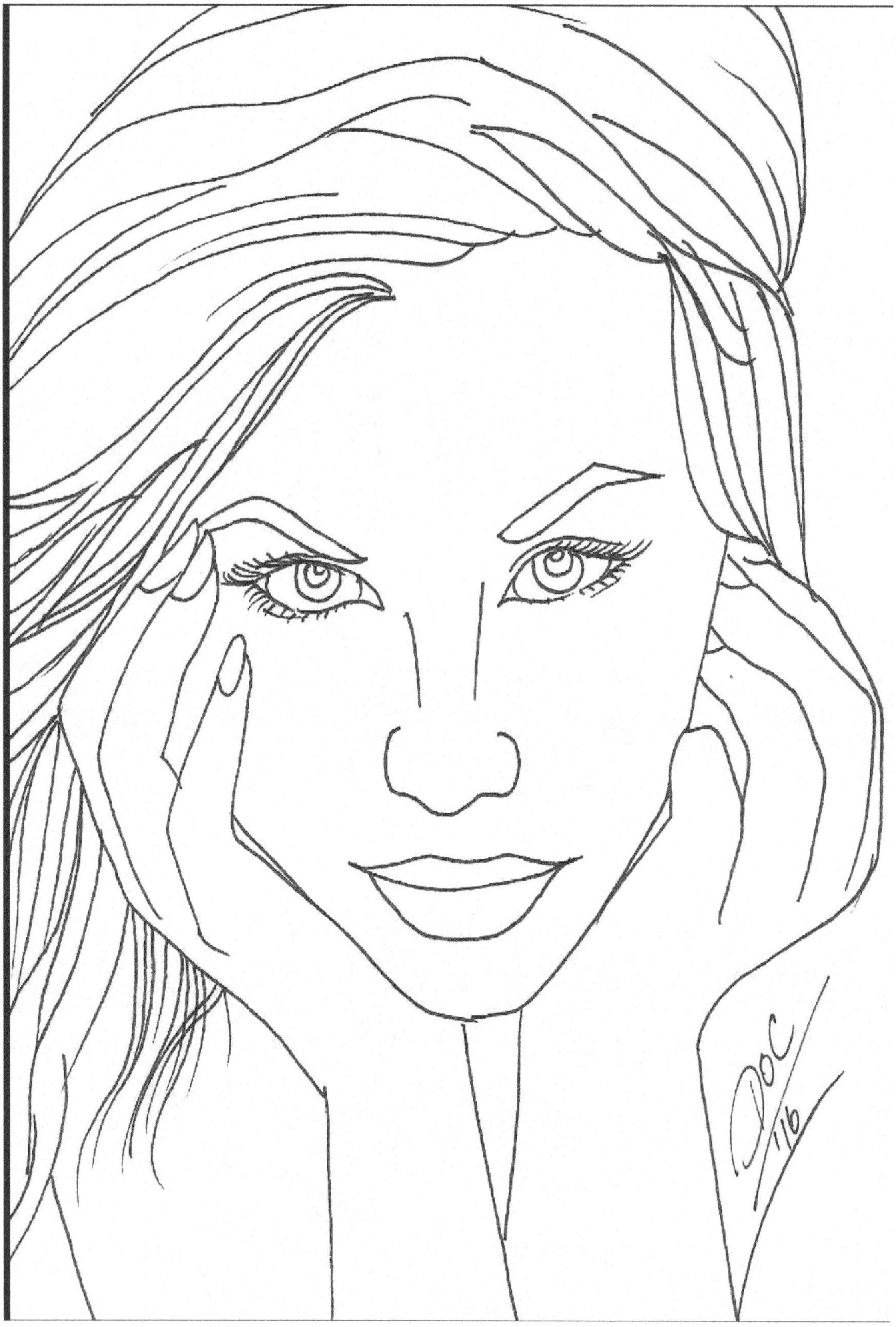
Doc '16

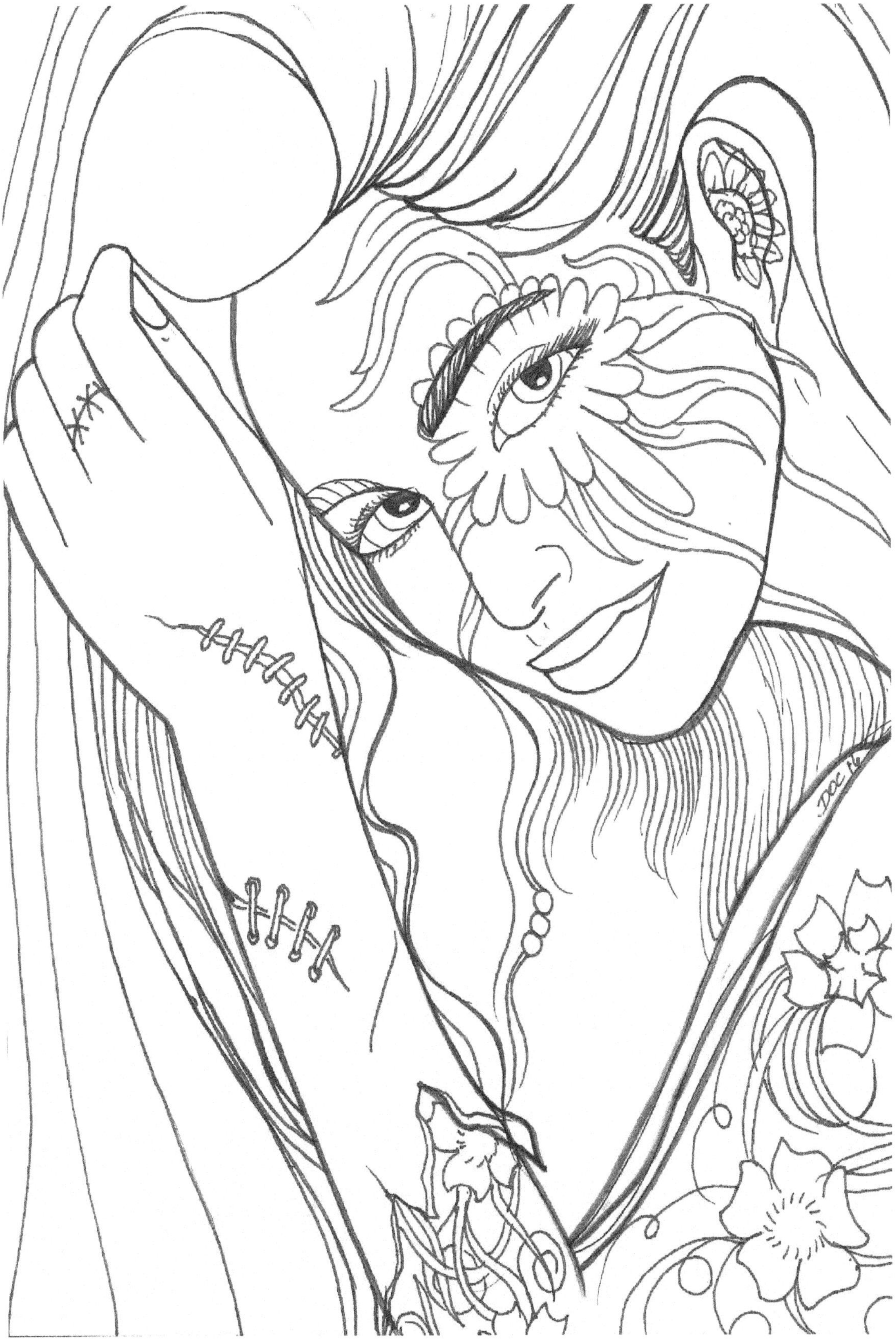

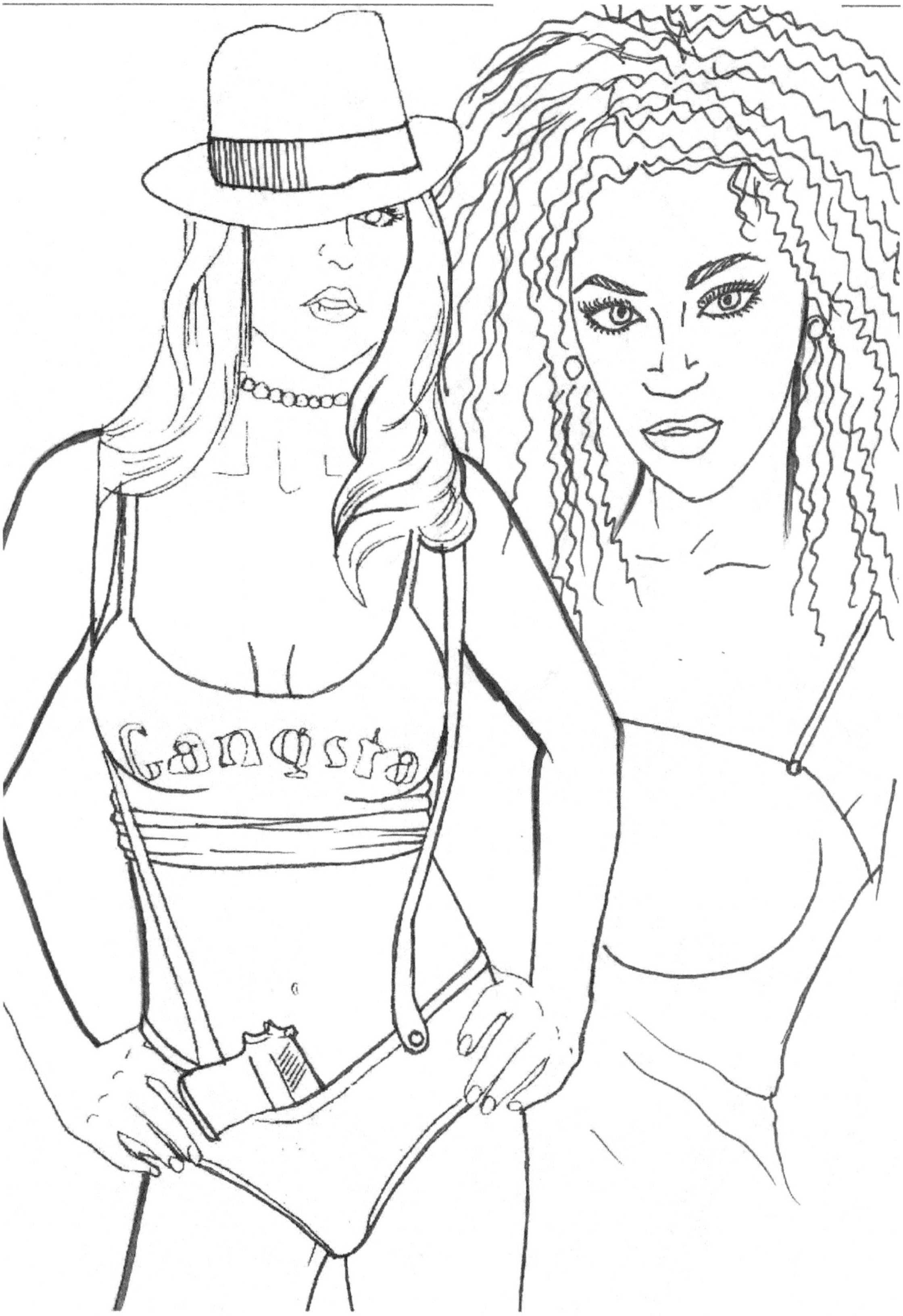
Gangsta

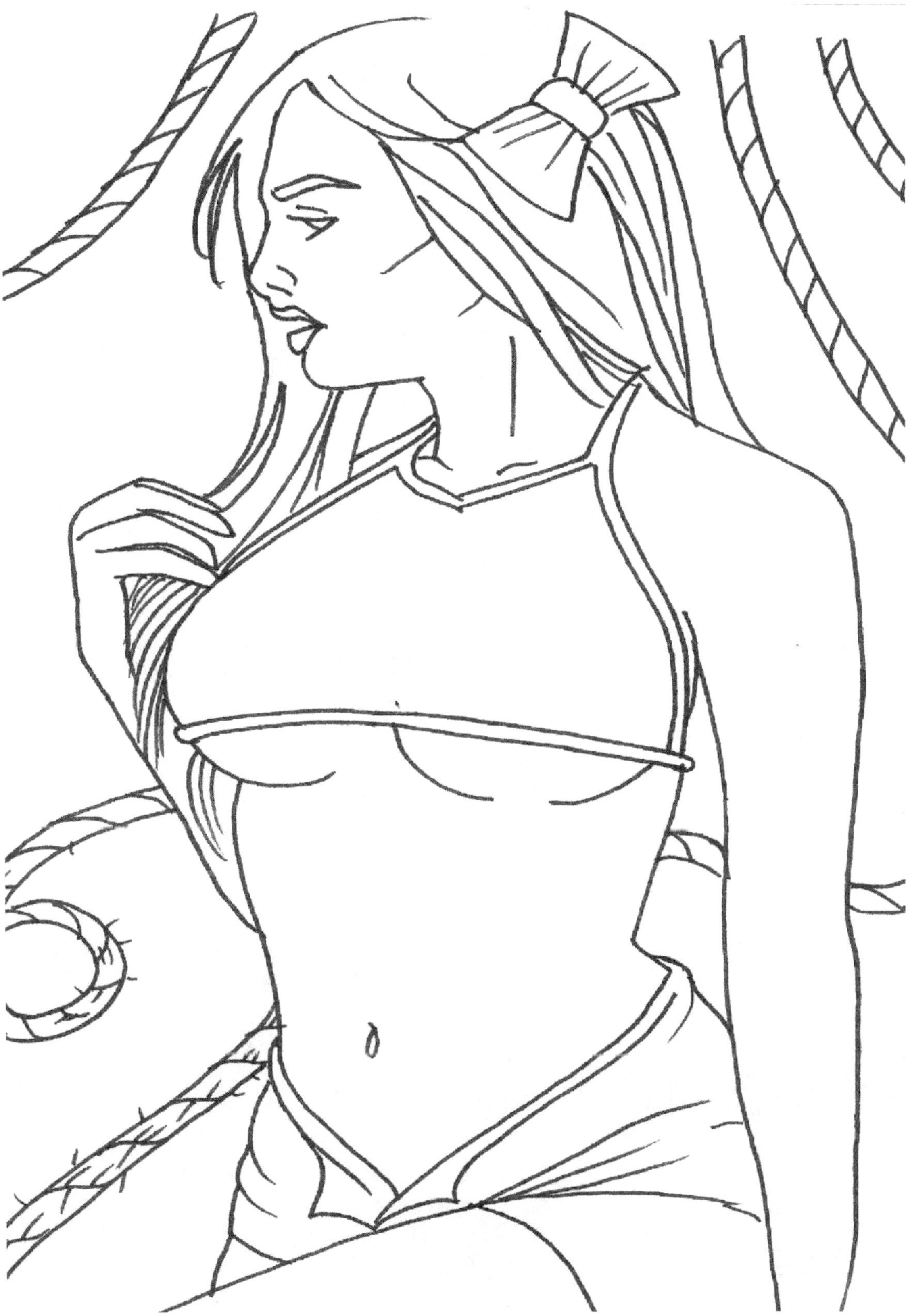

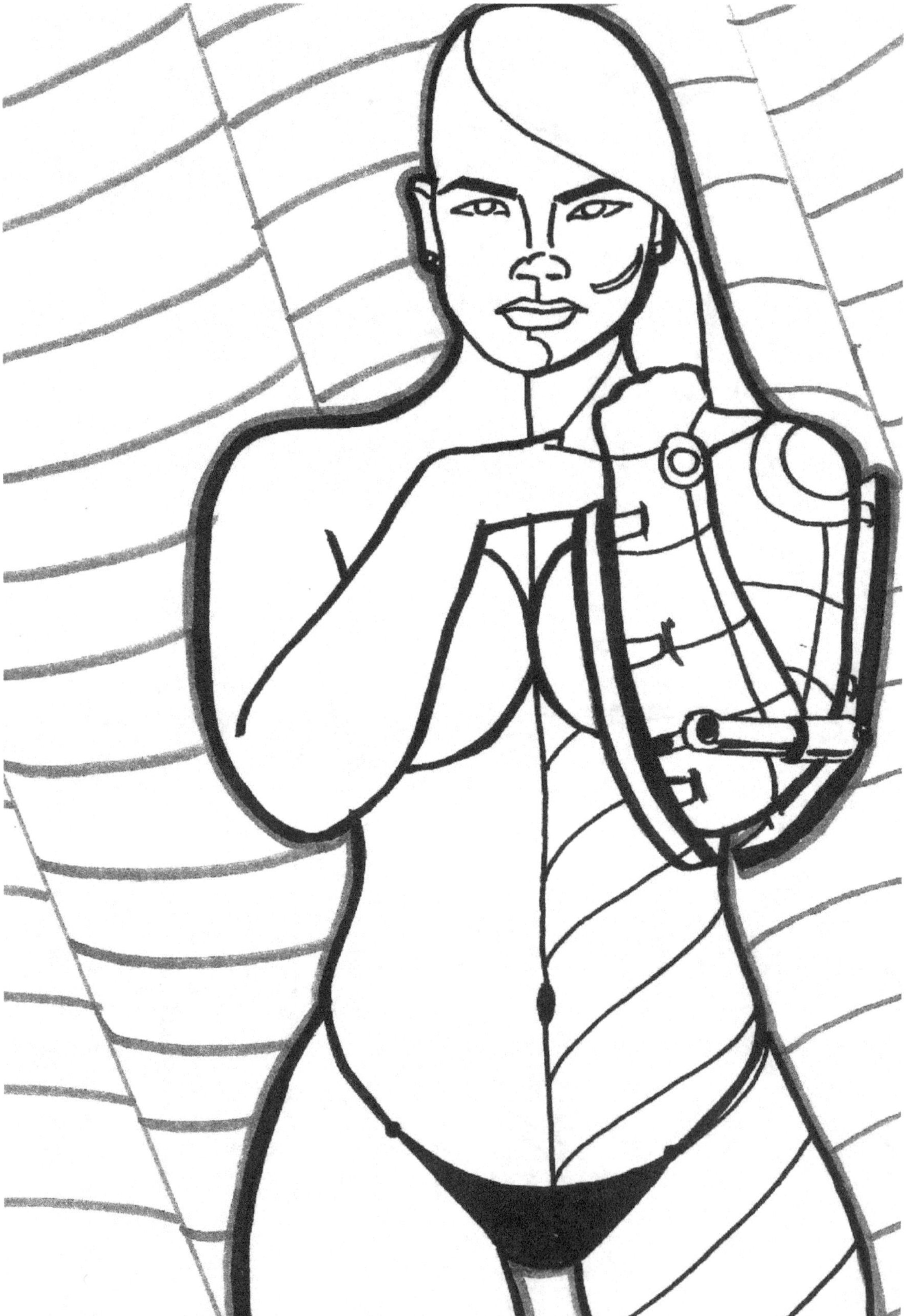

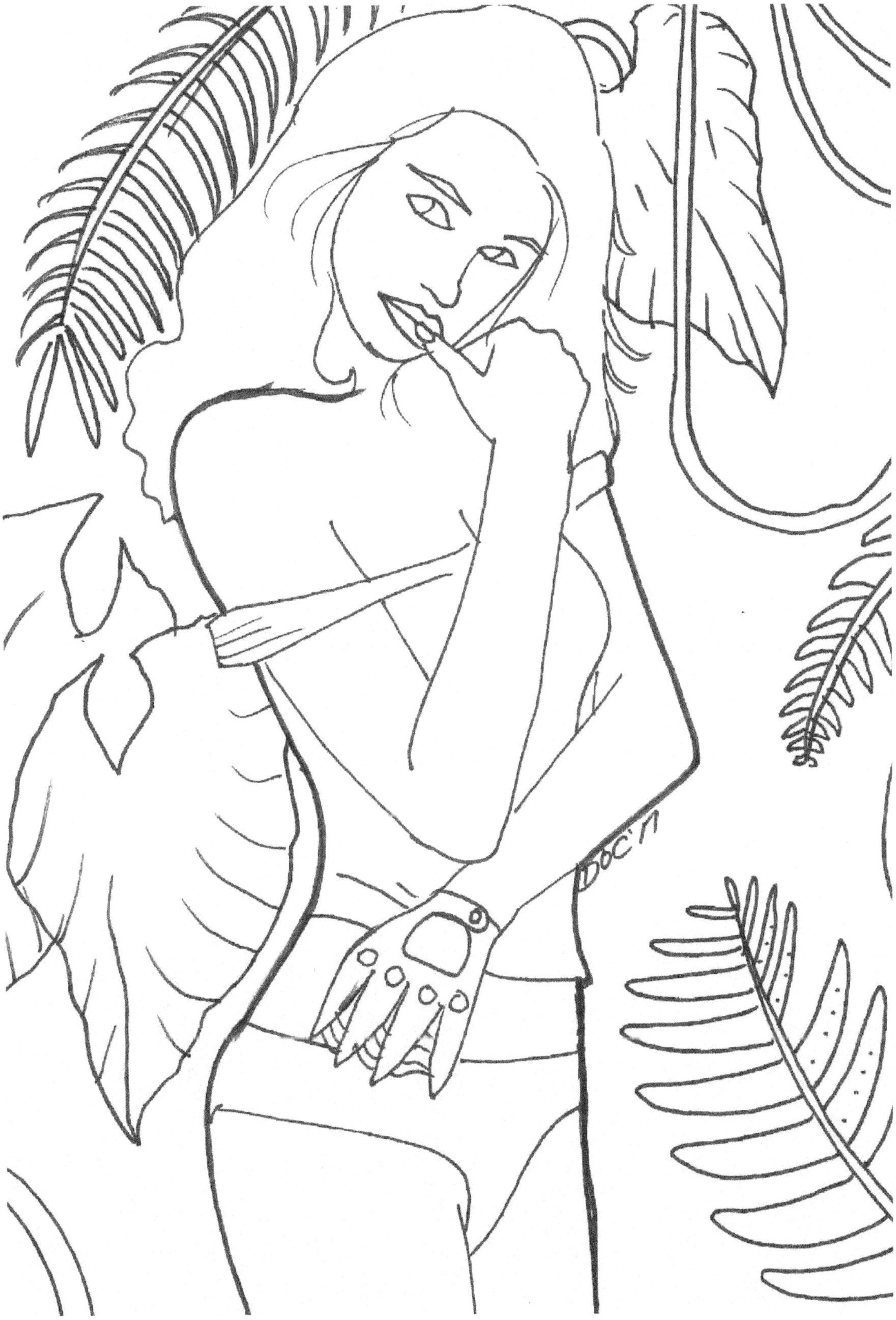

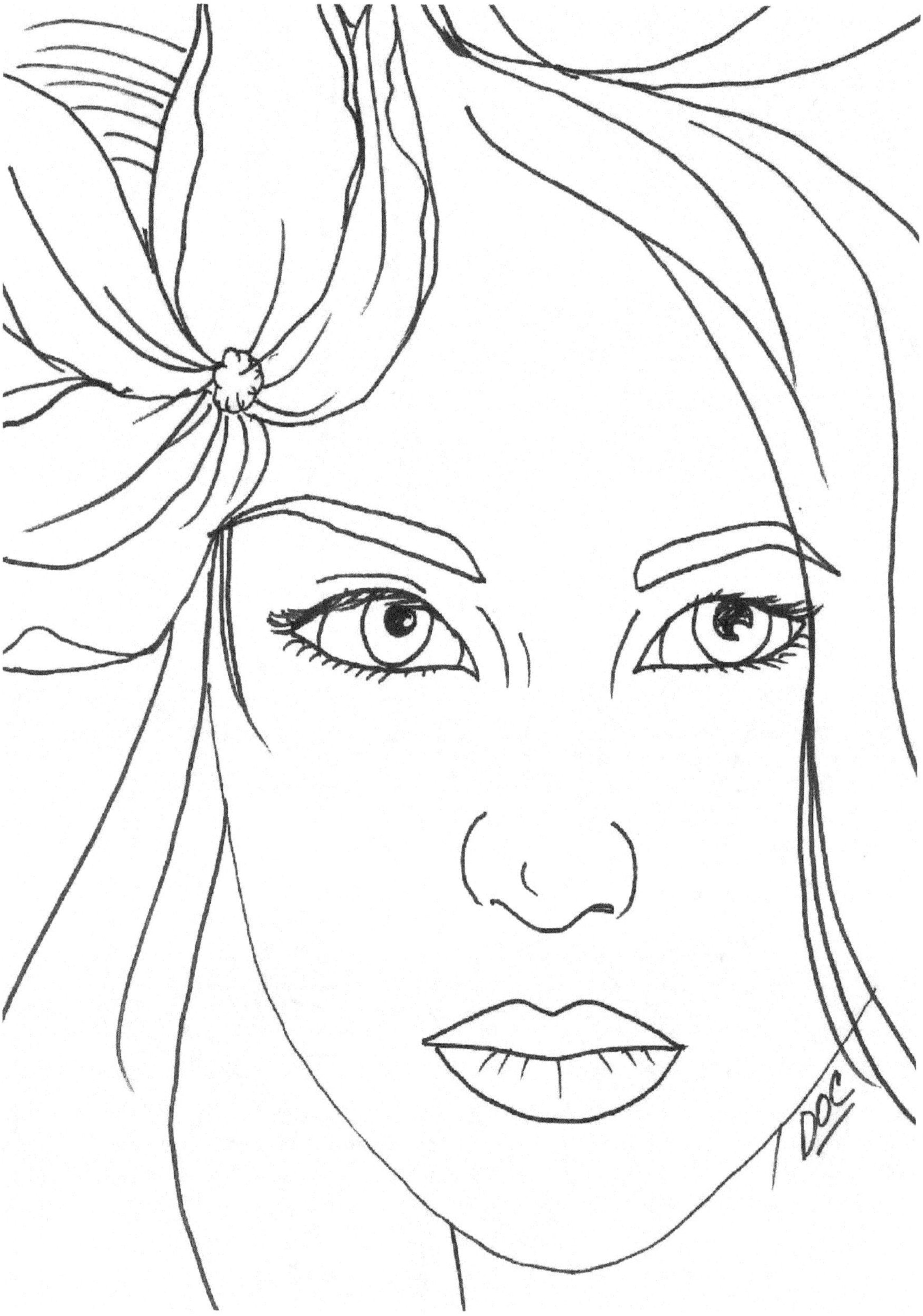
DOC

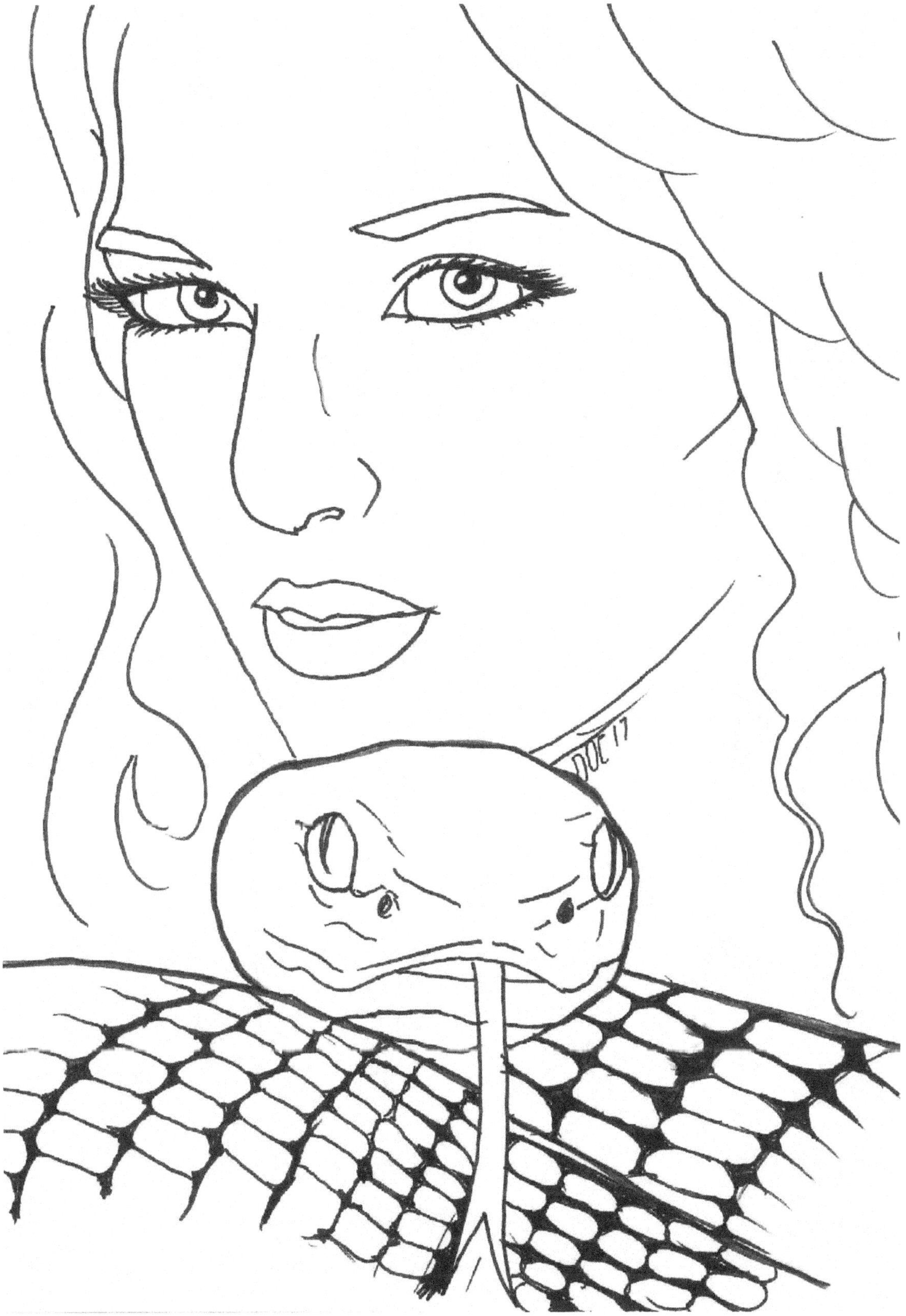
DOC 17

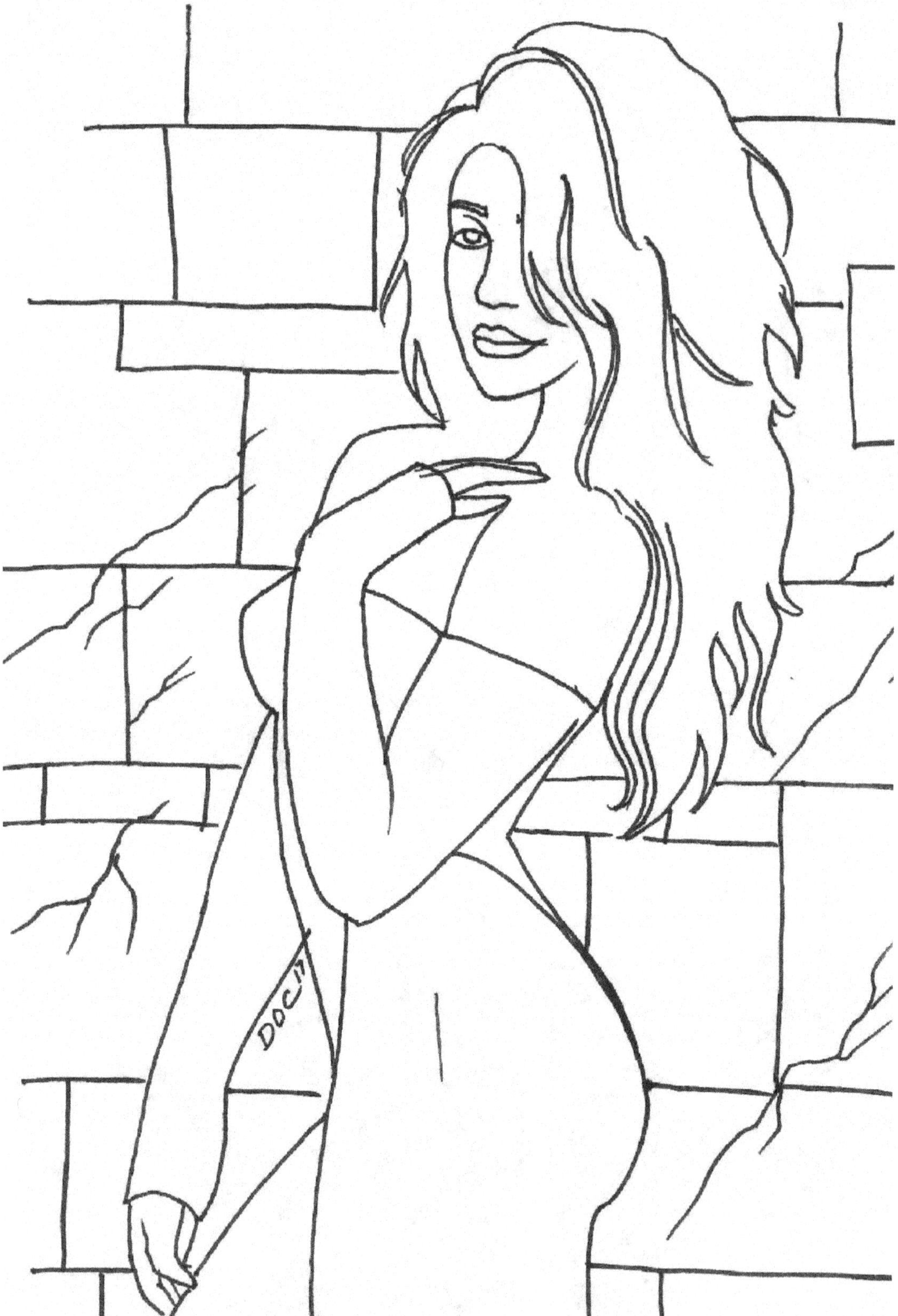

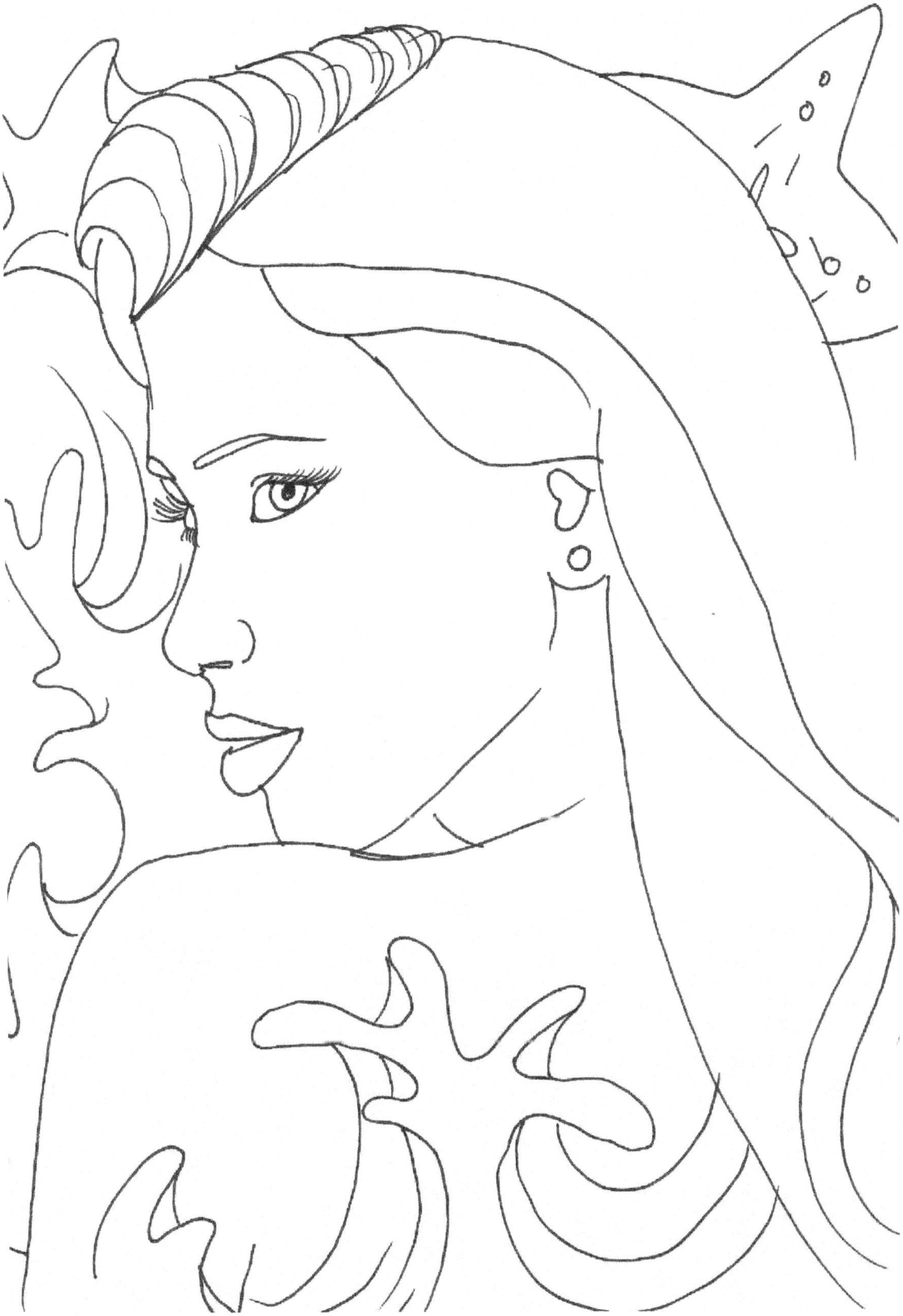

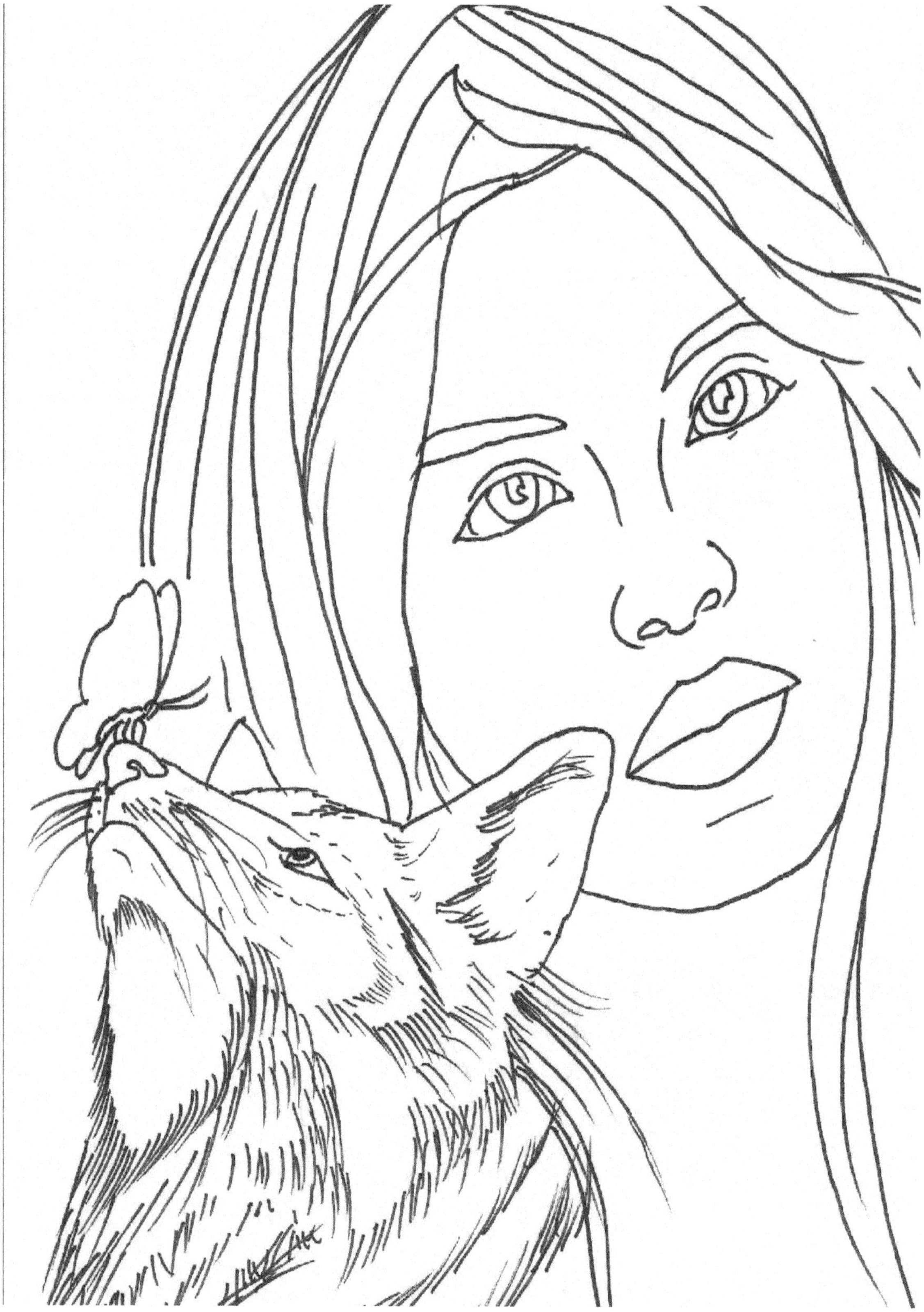

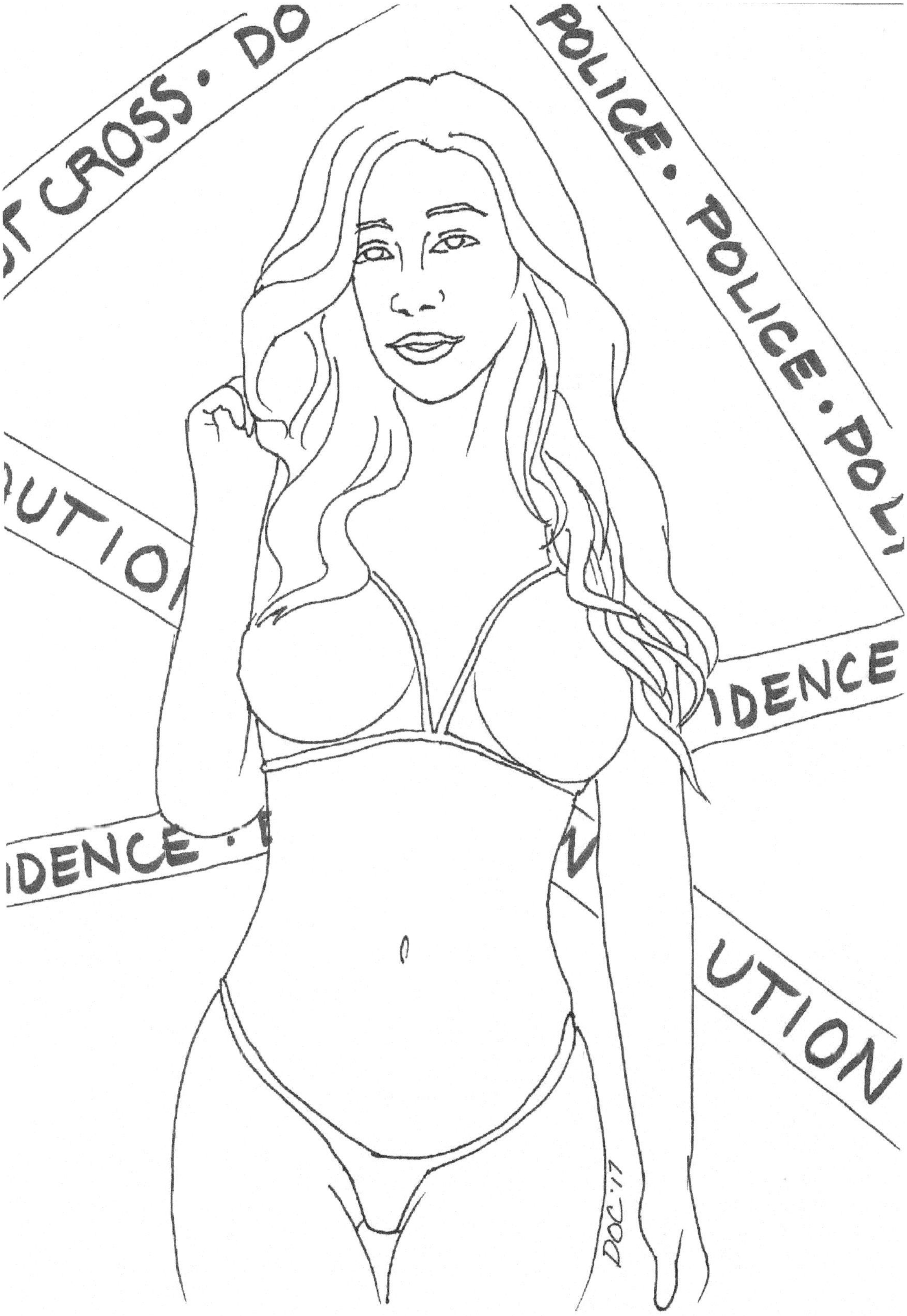
ST CROSS • DO
POLICE • POLICE • POLI
UTION
IDENCE
IDENCE • E
UTION
DOC '17

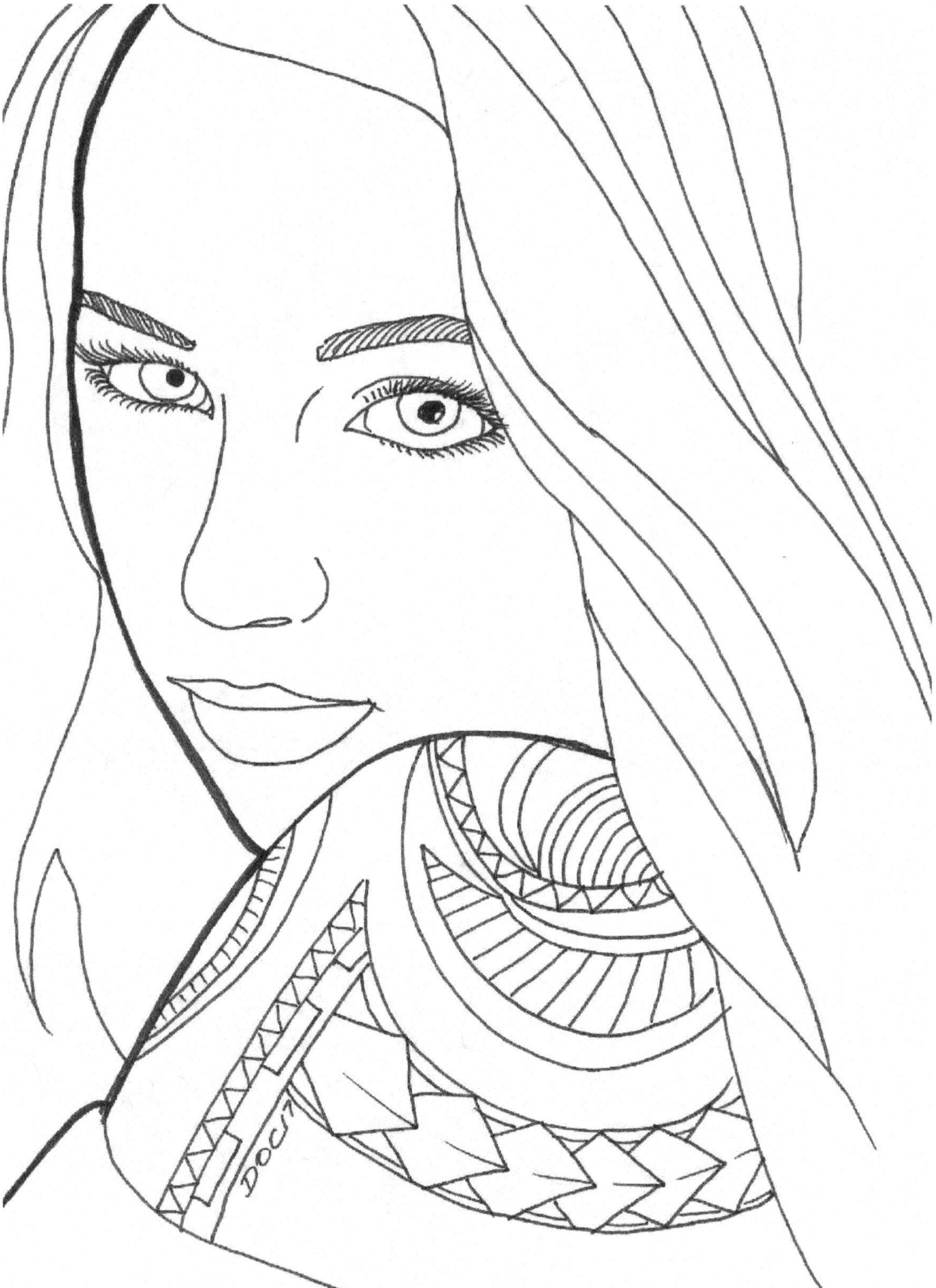

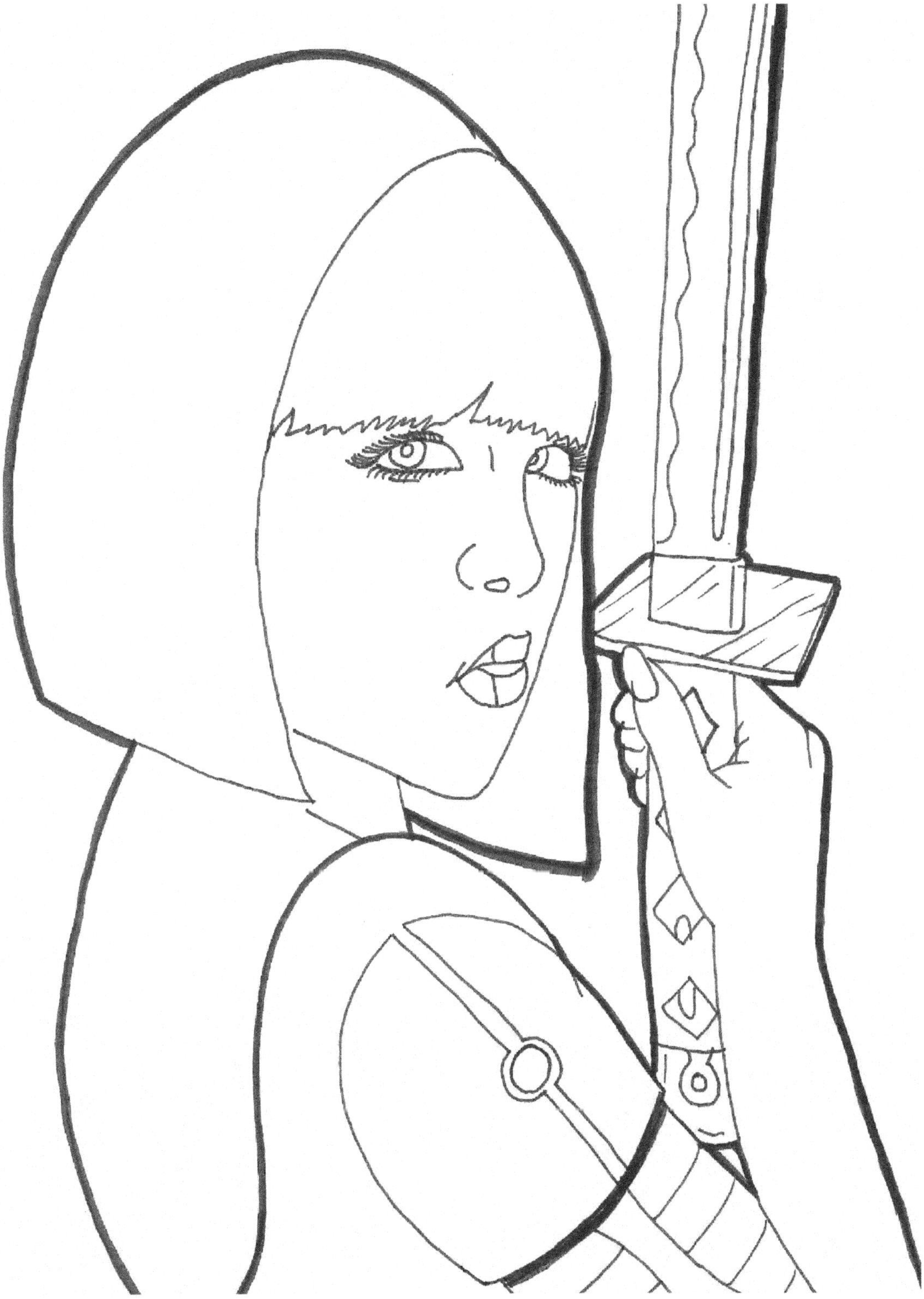

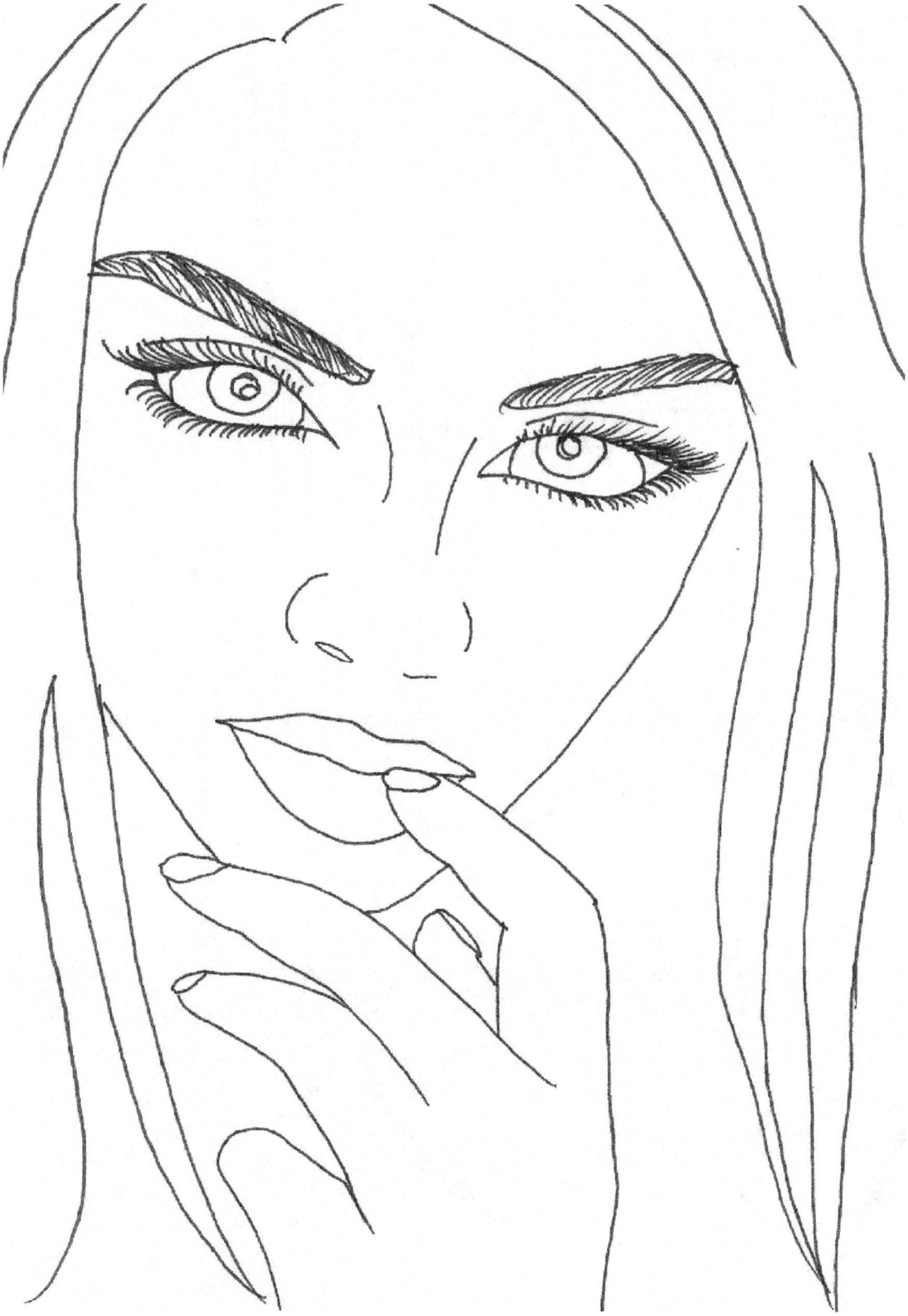

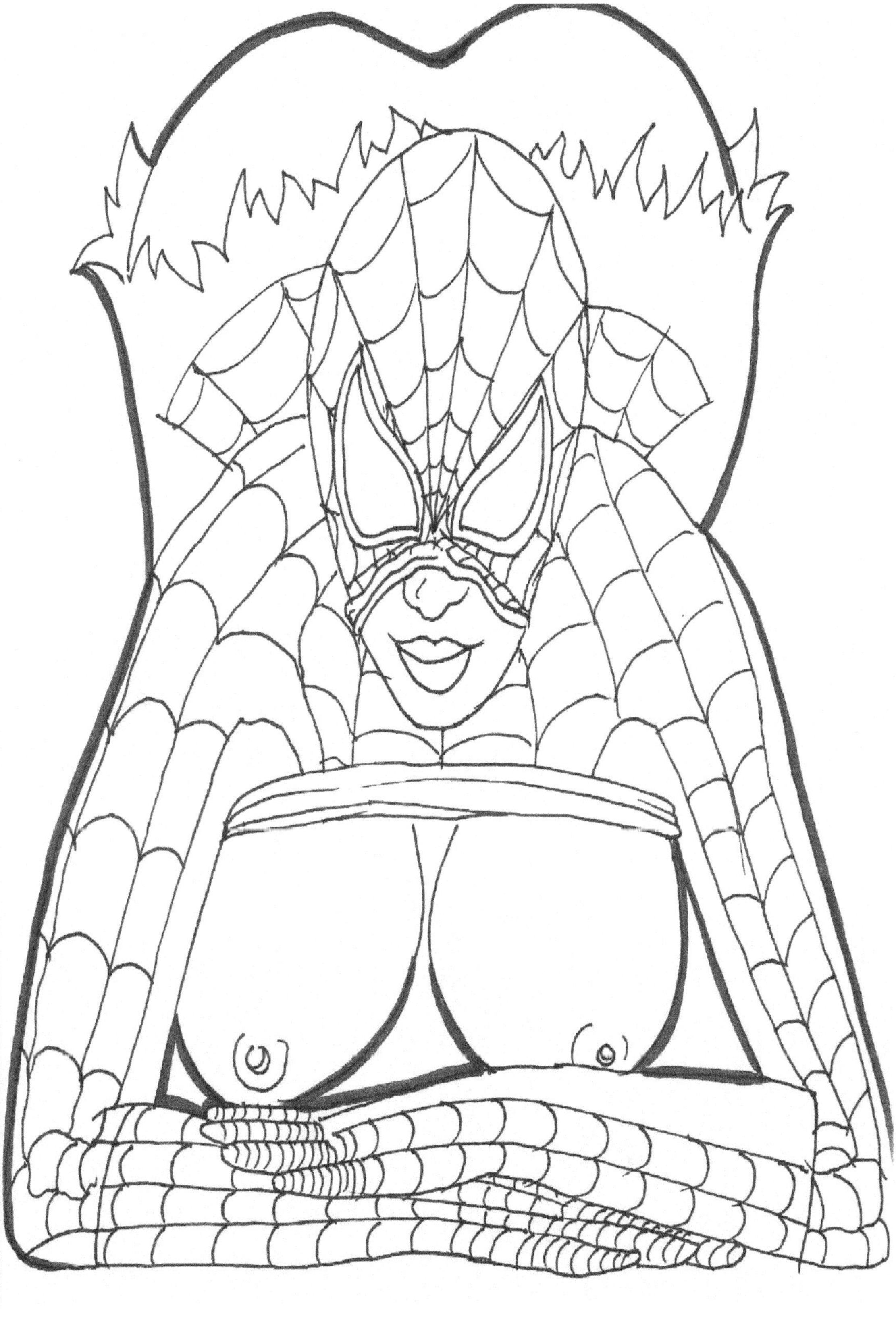

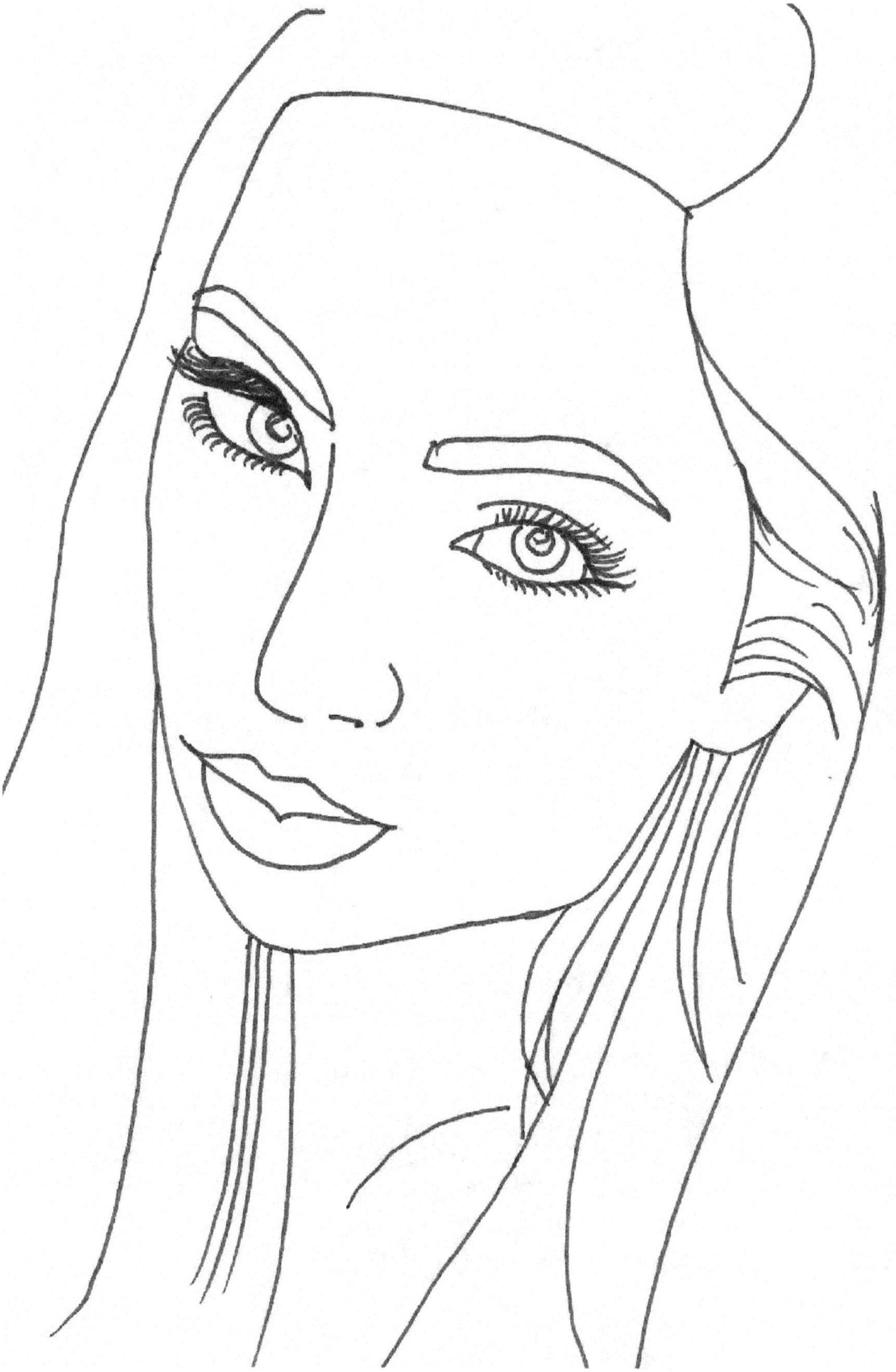

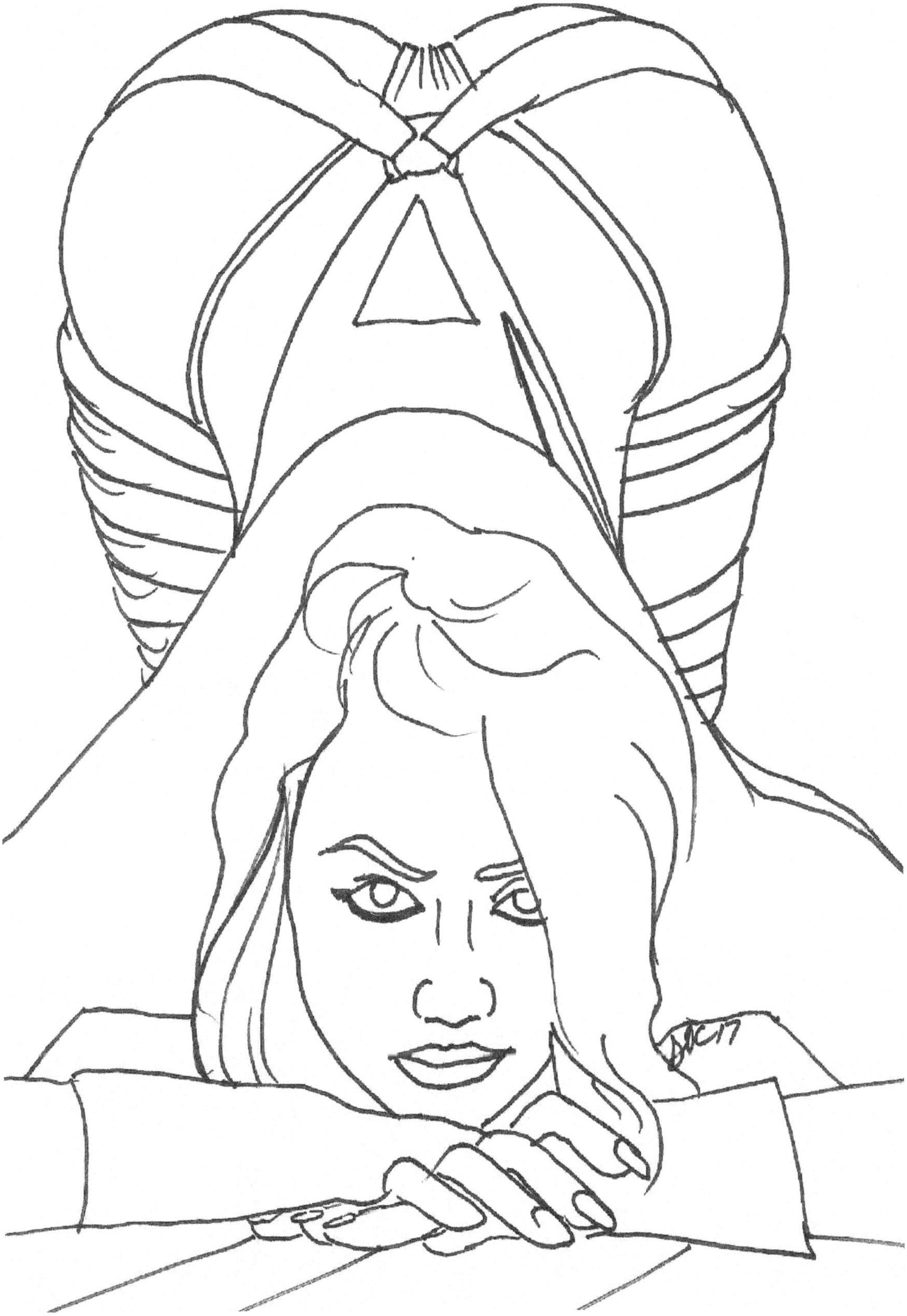

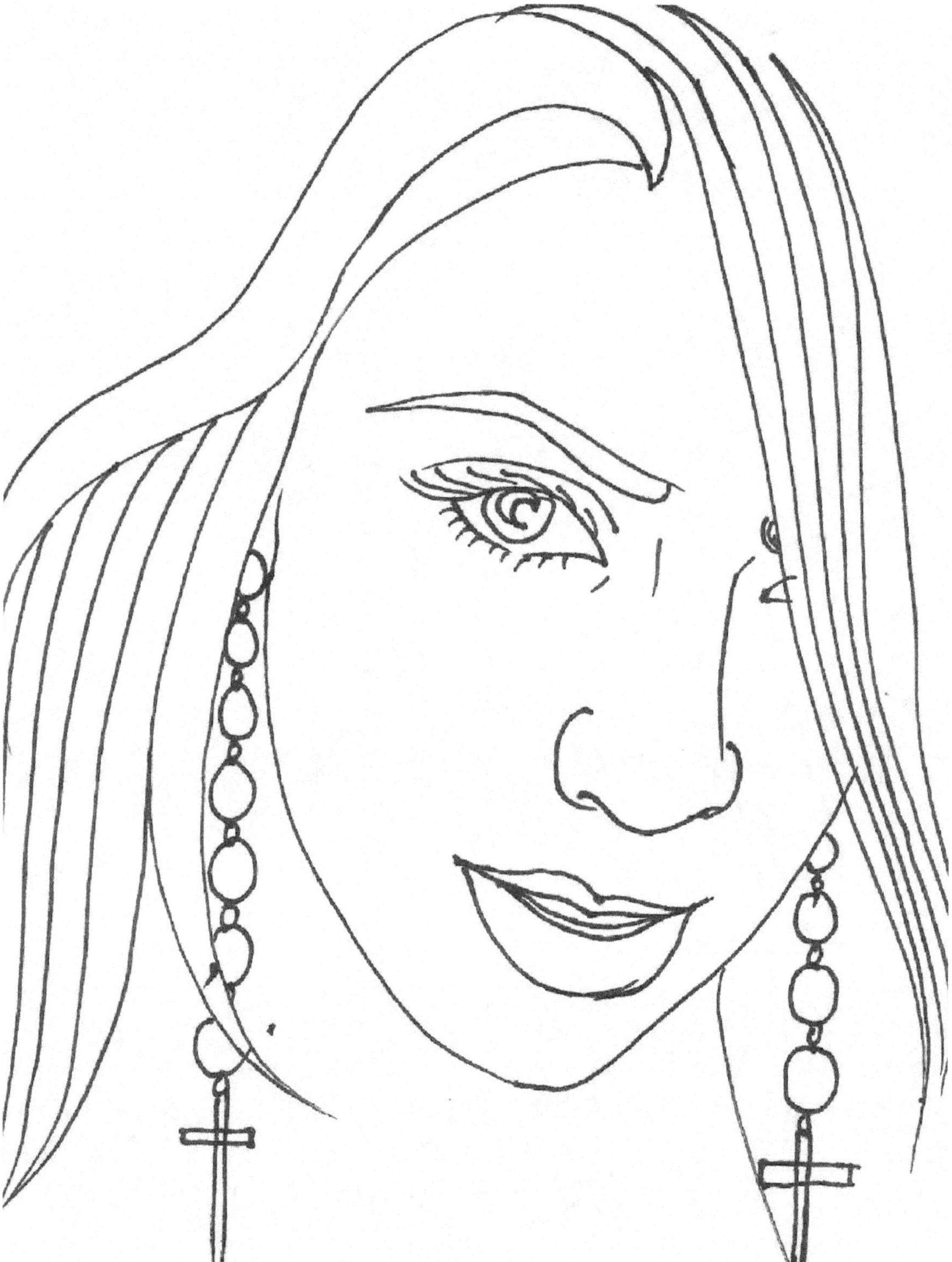

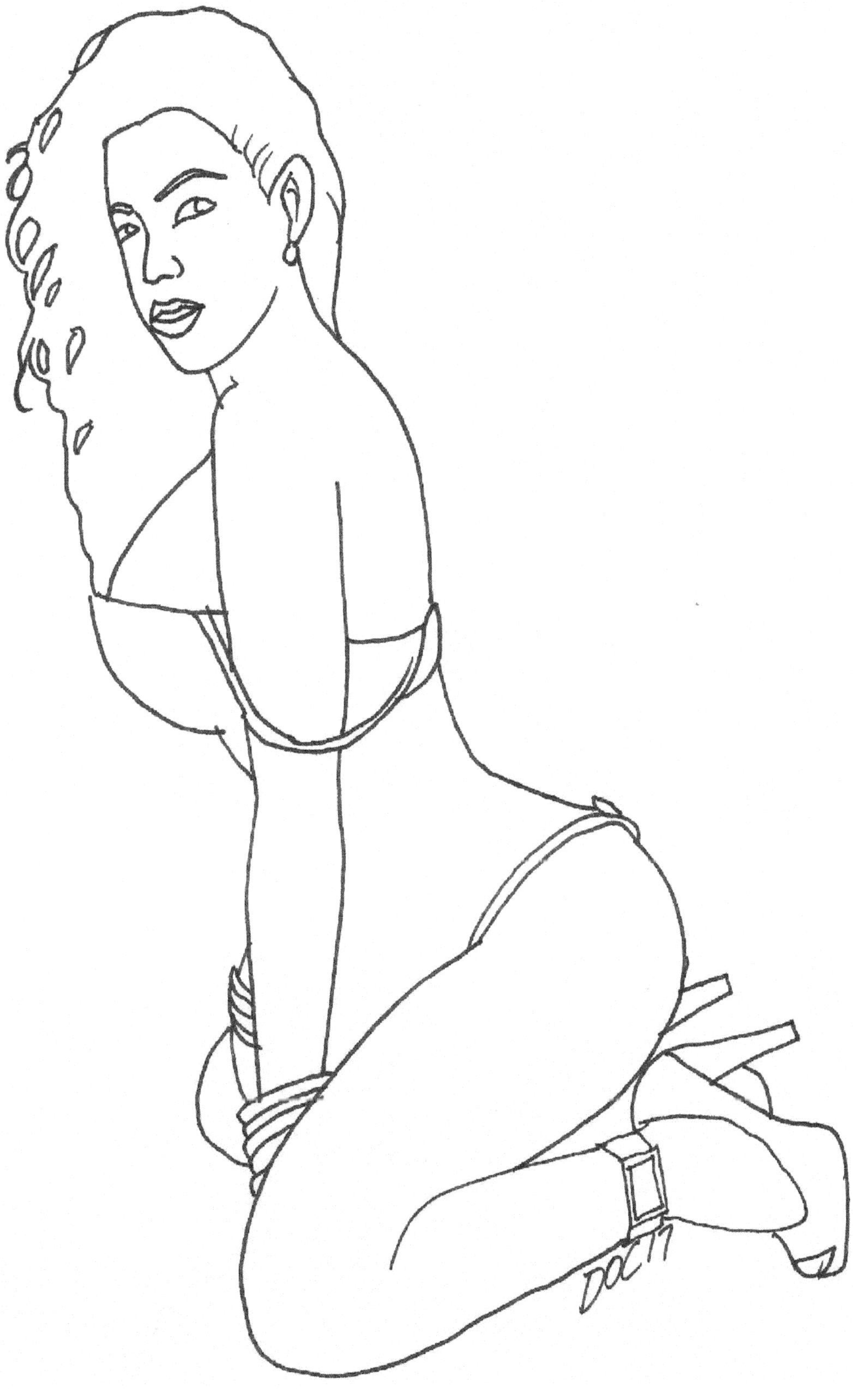
DOC17

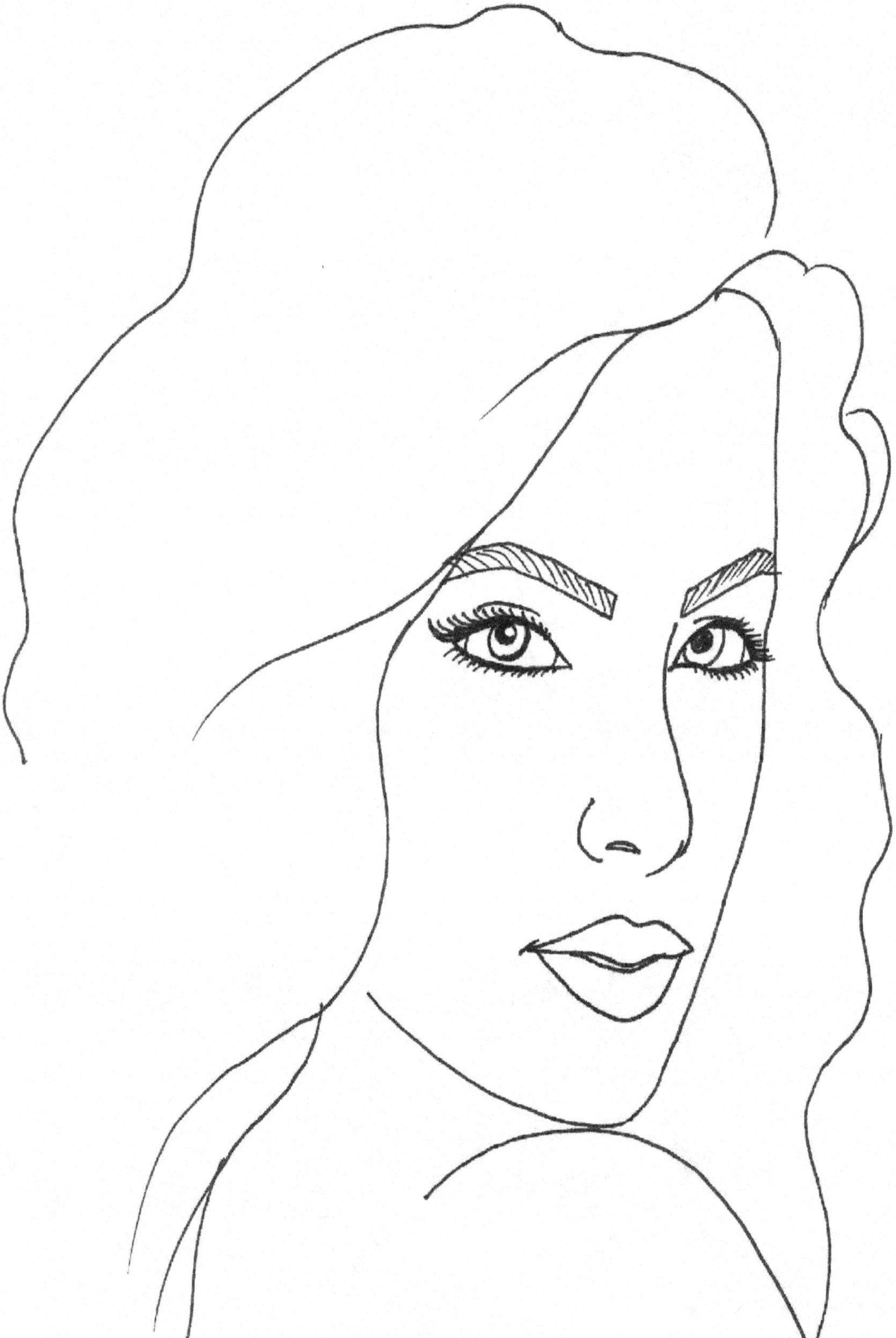

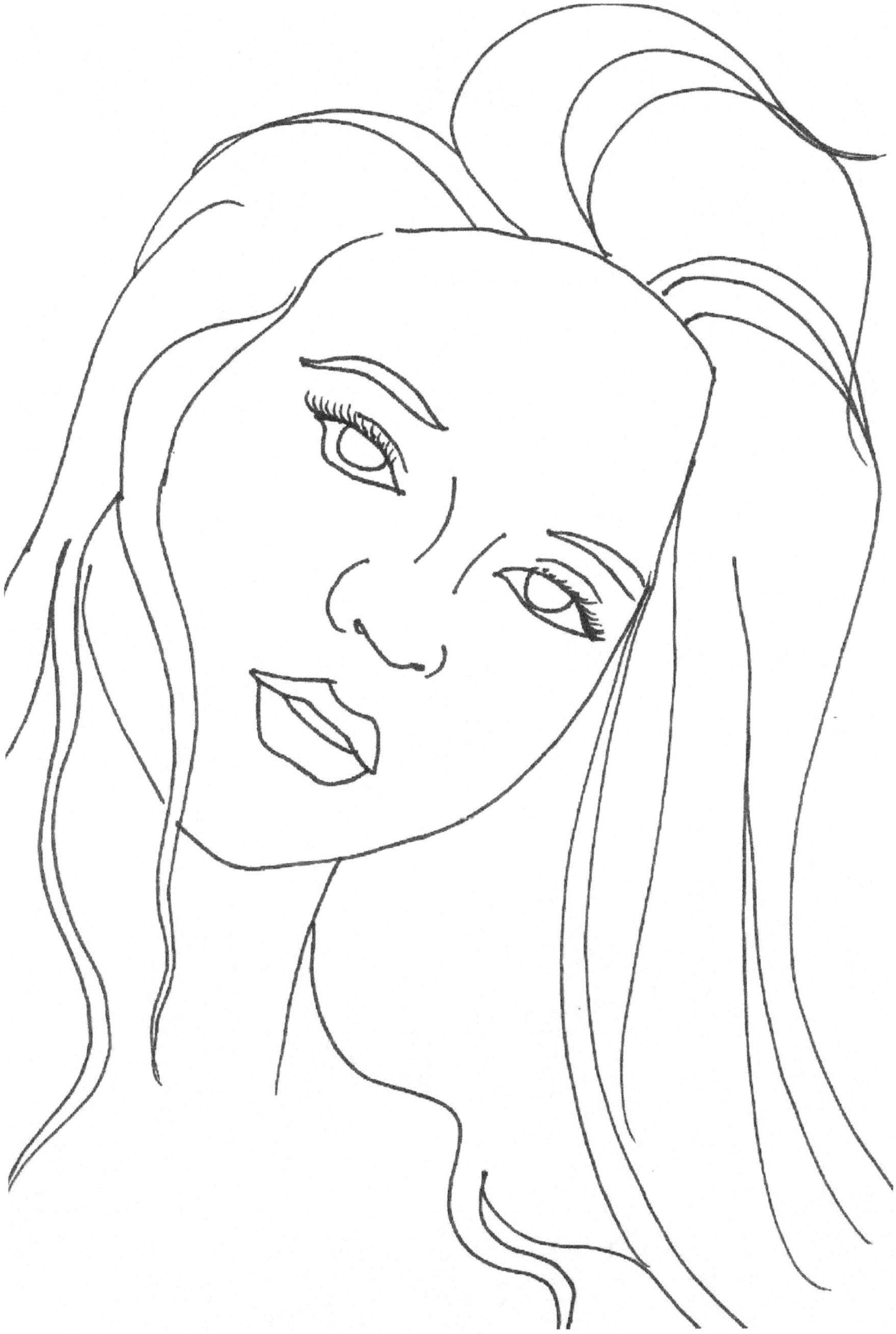

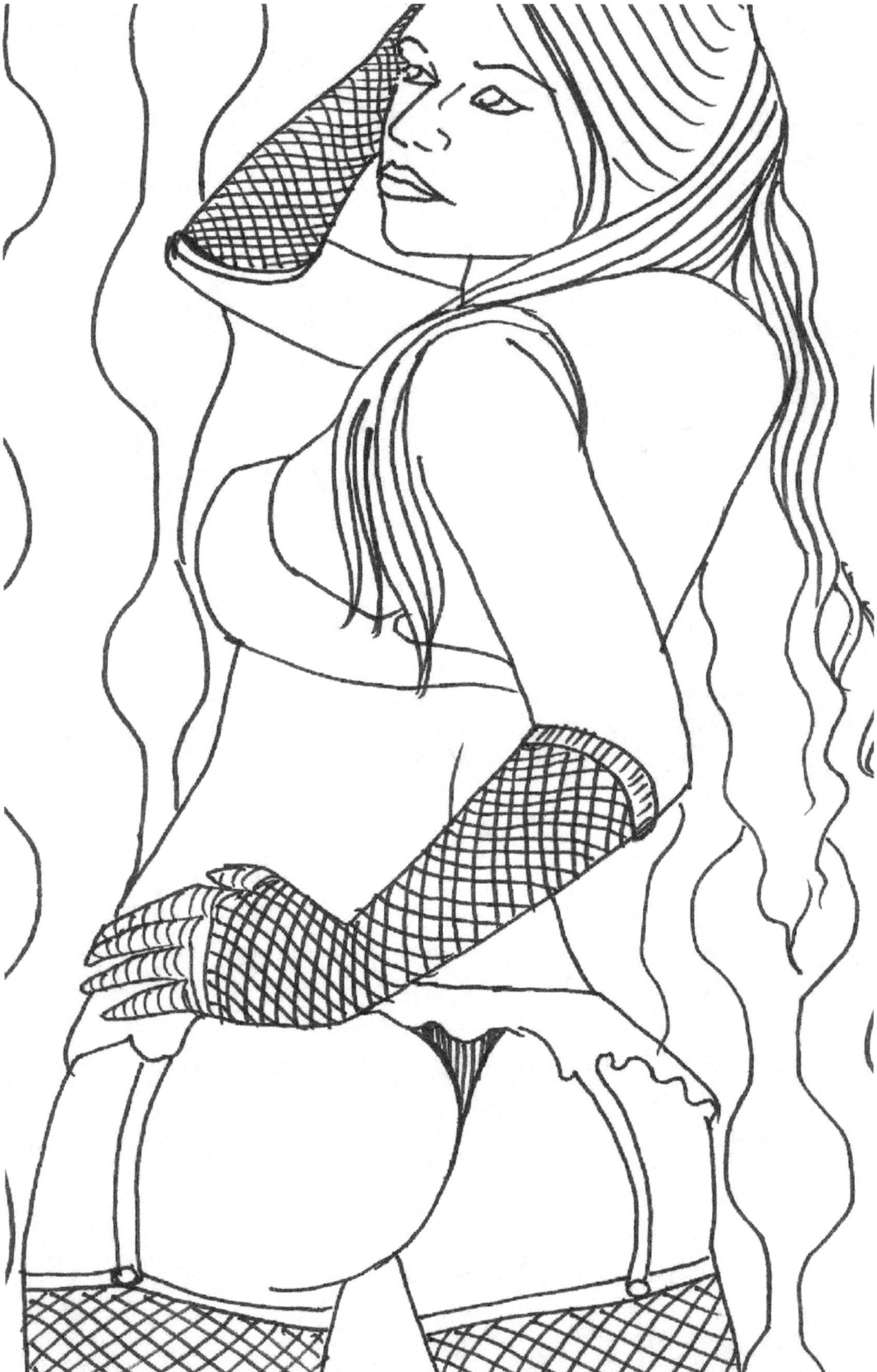

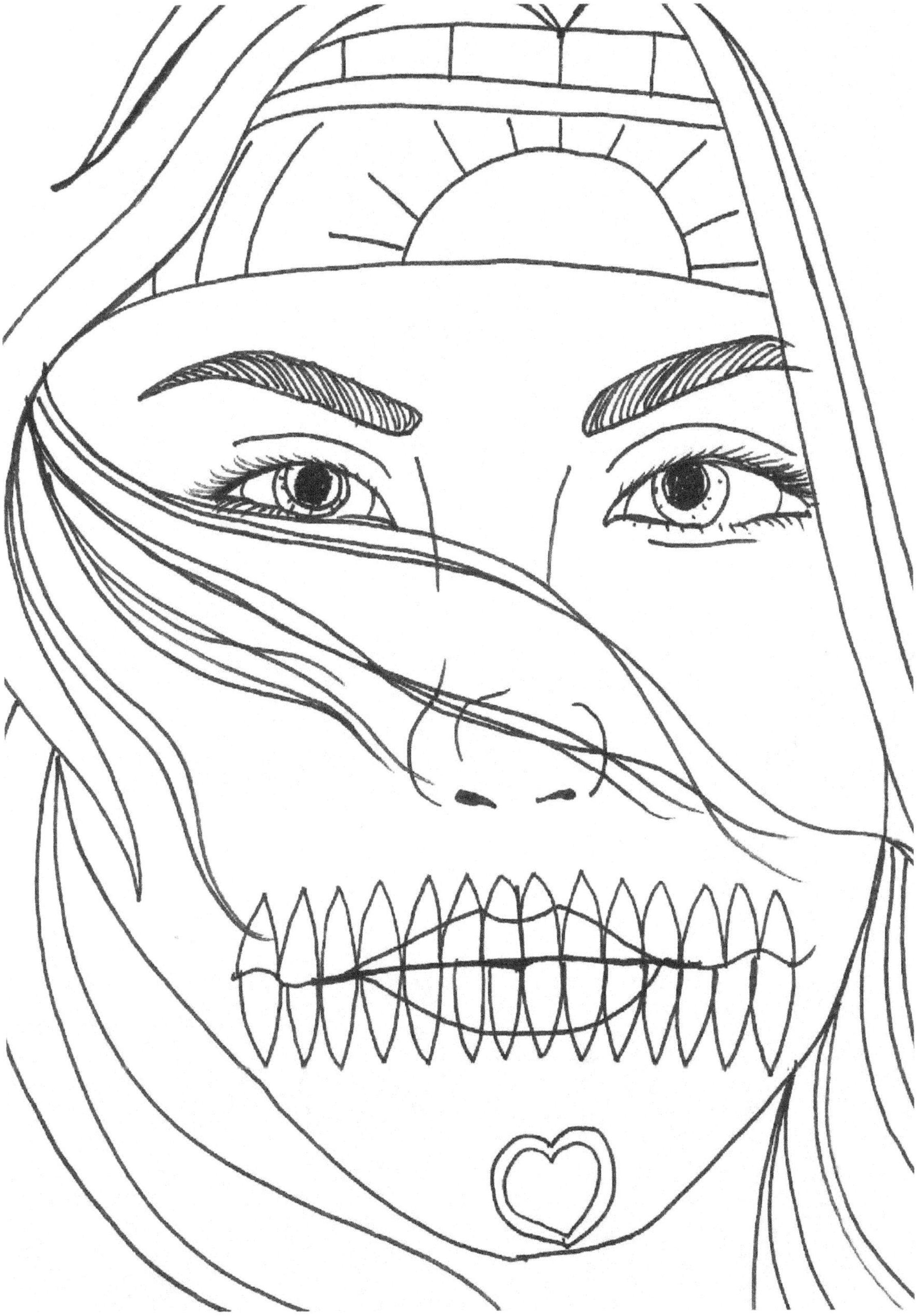

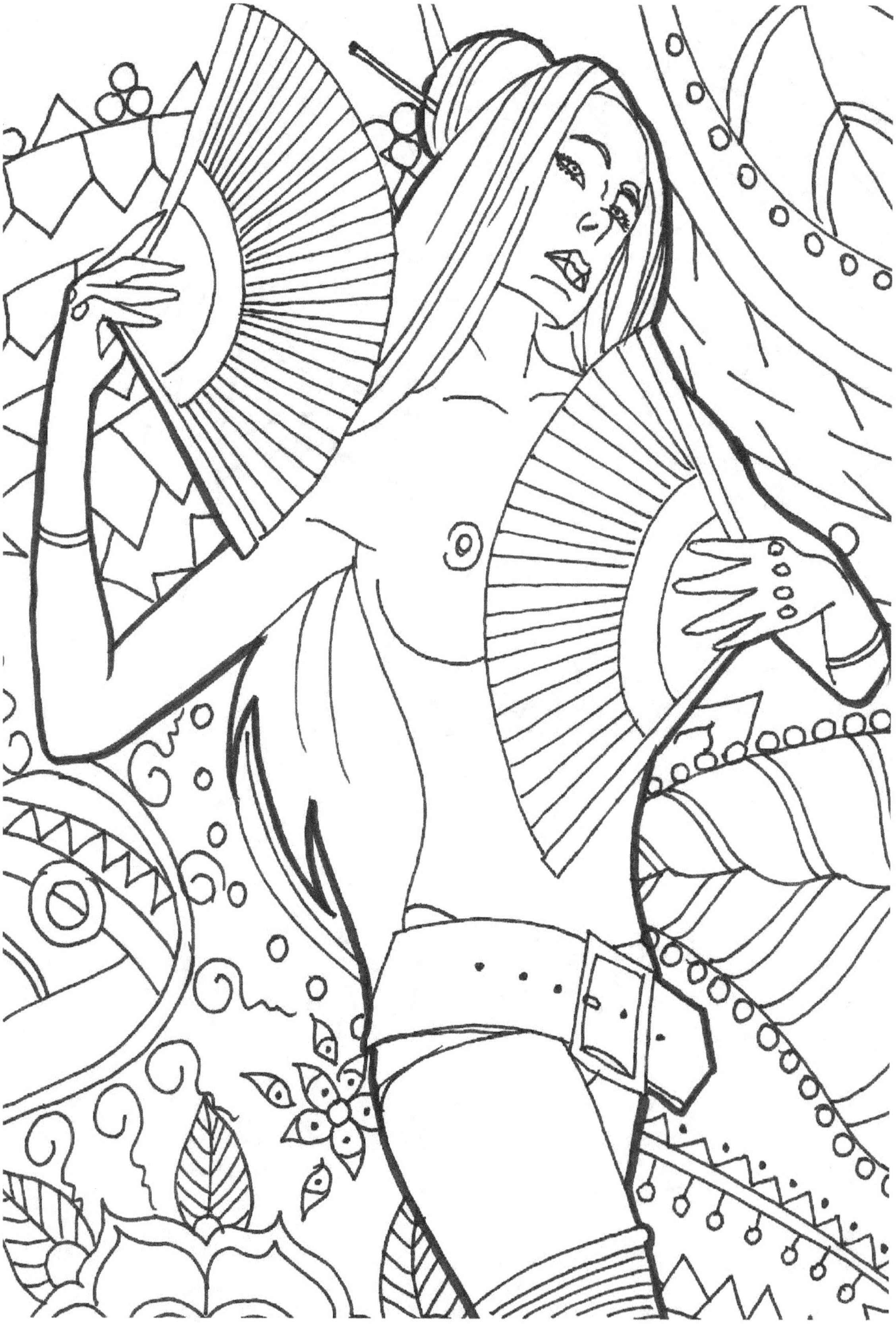

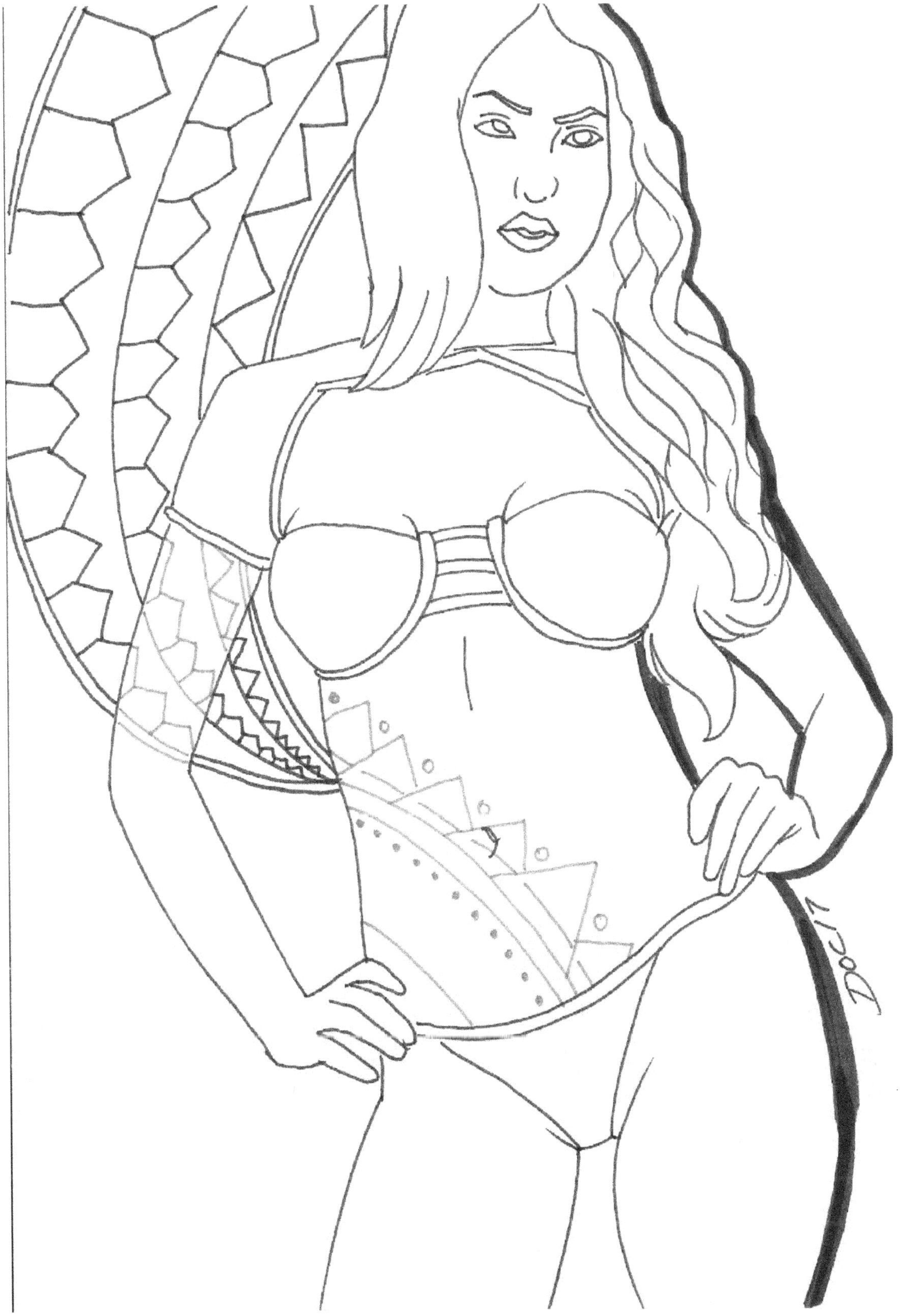
Doc17

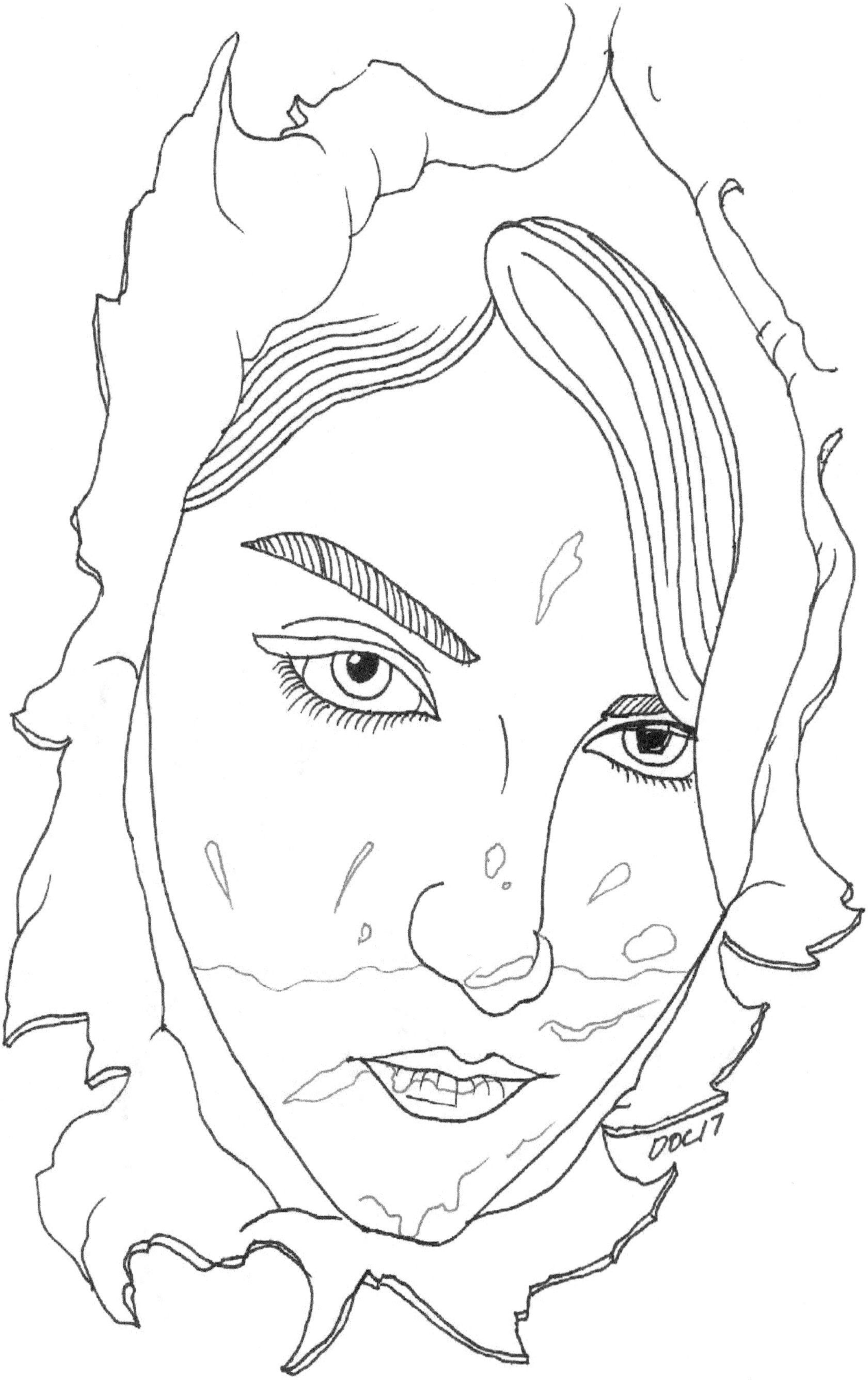
DOC17

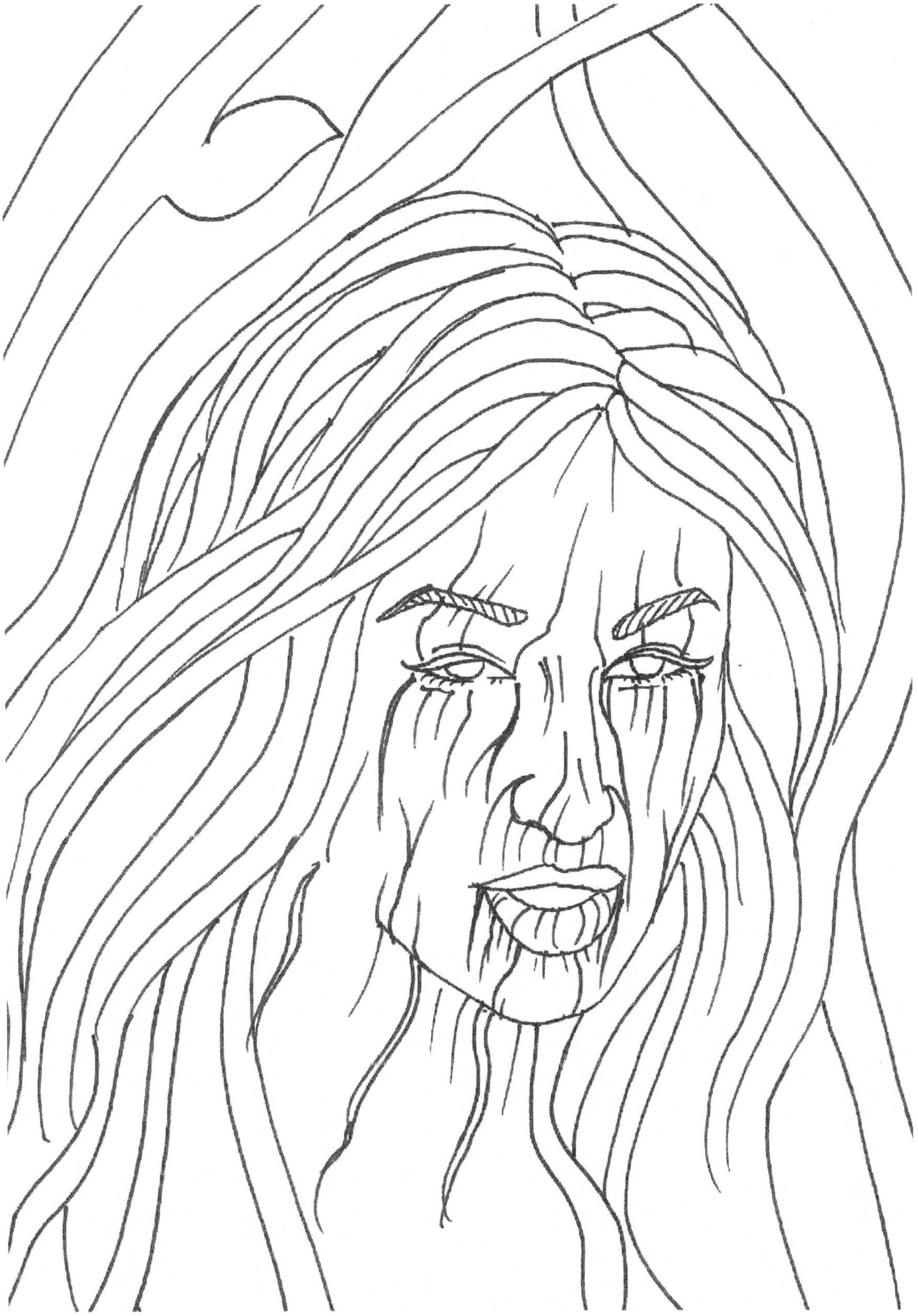

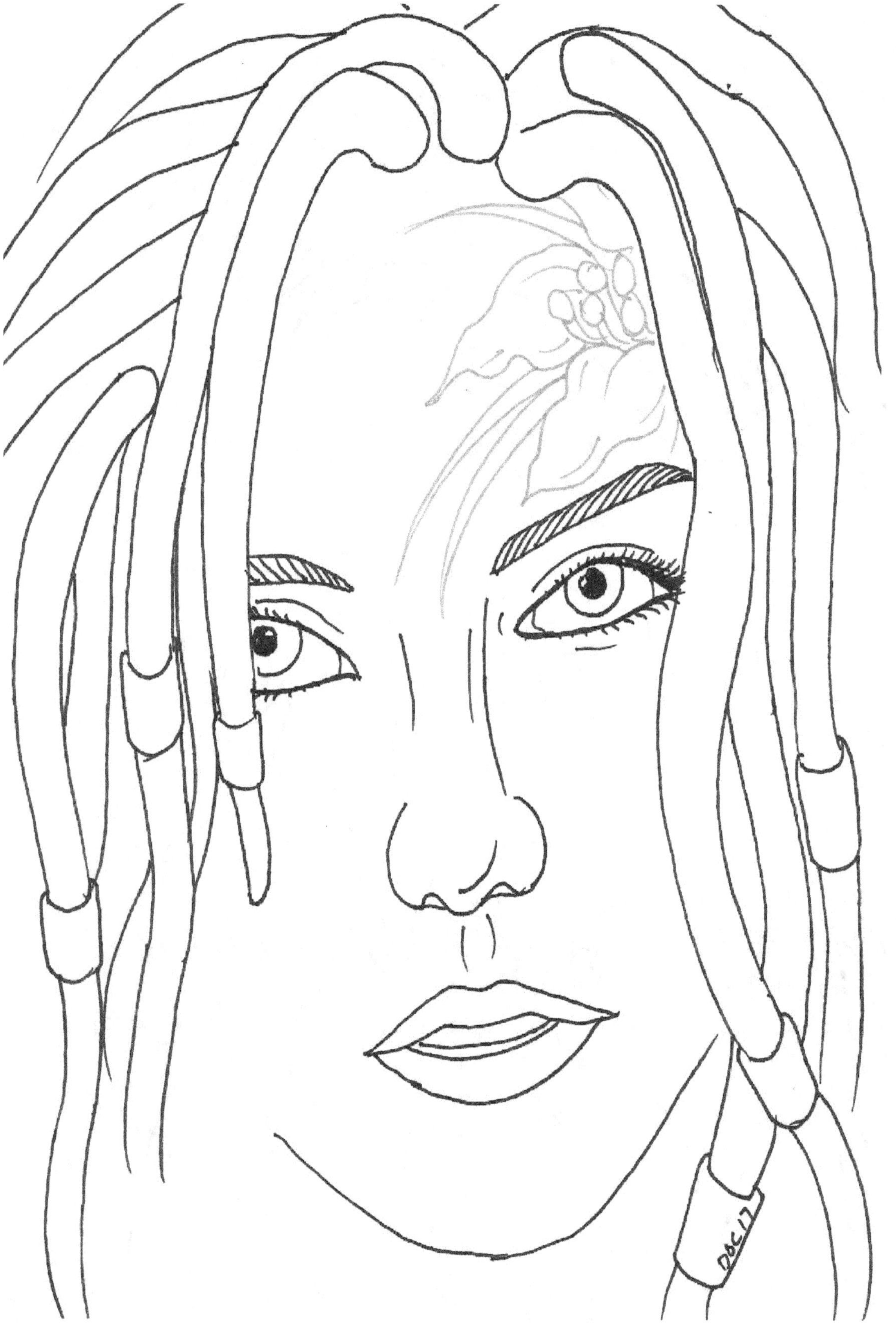
DOC17

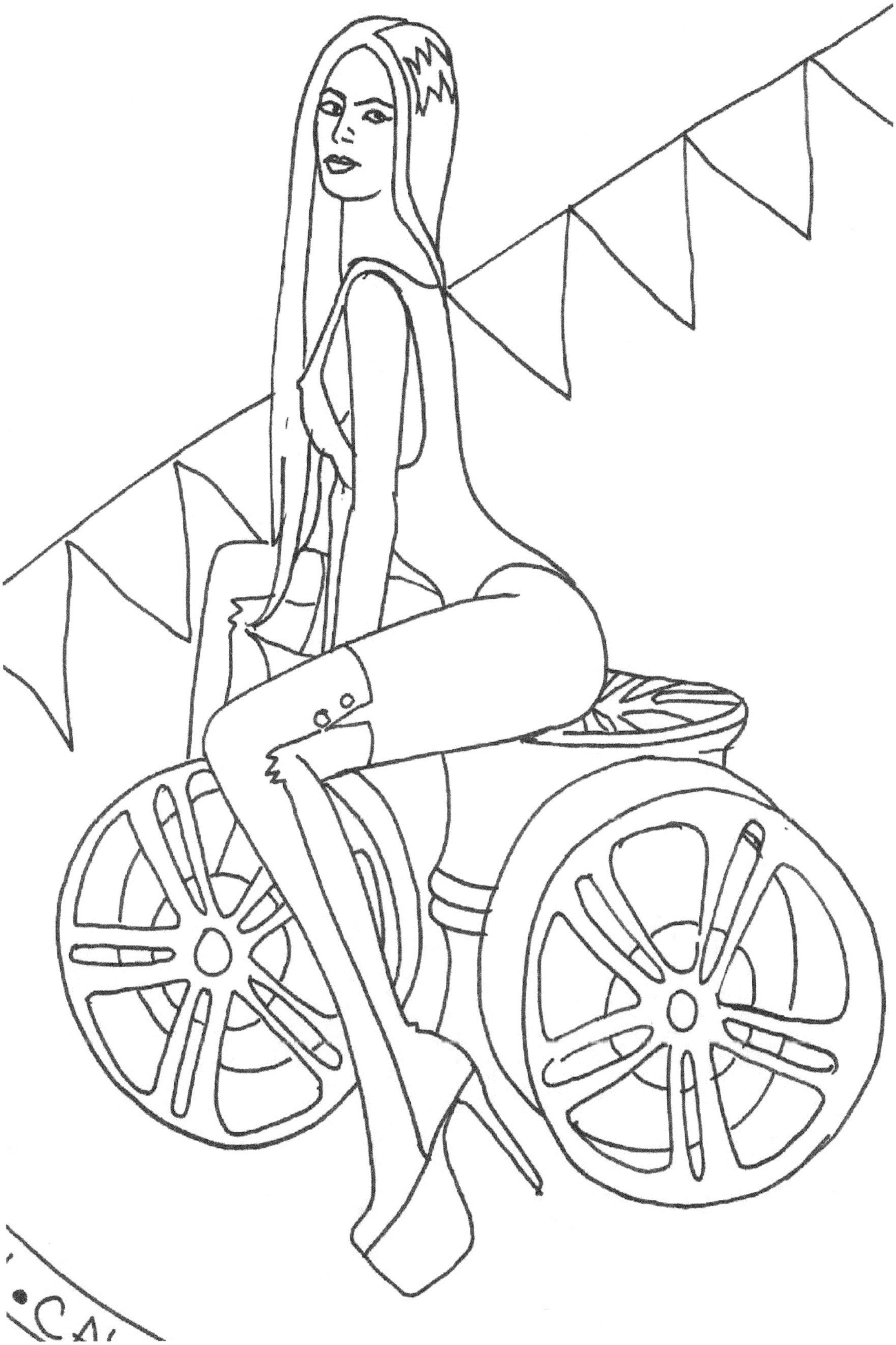

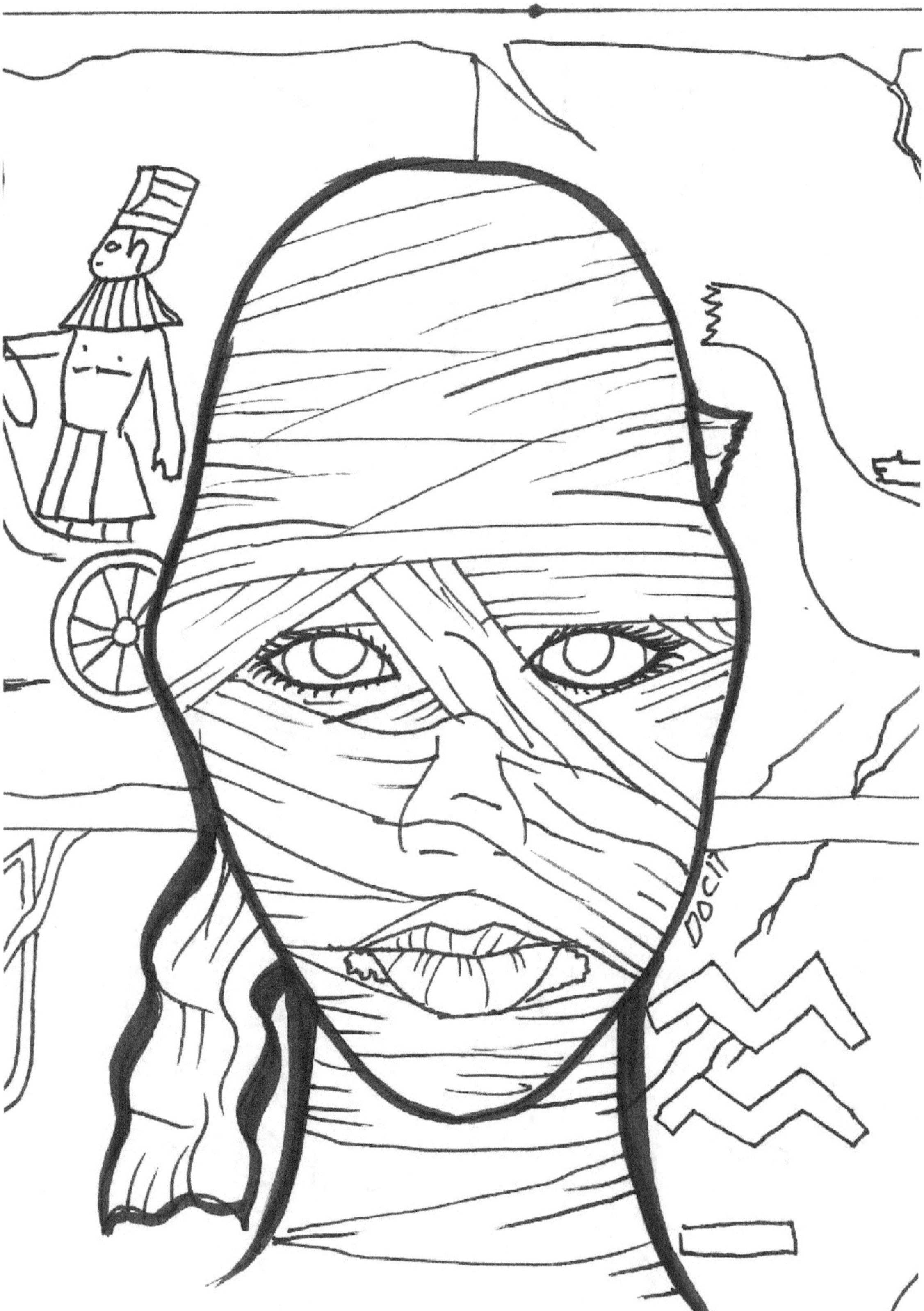
DOCIT

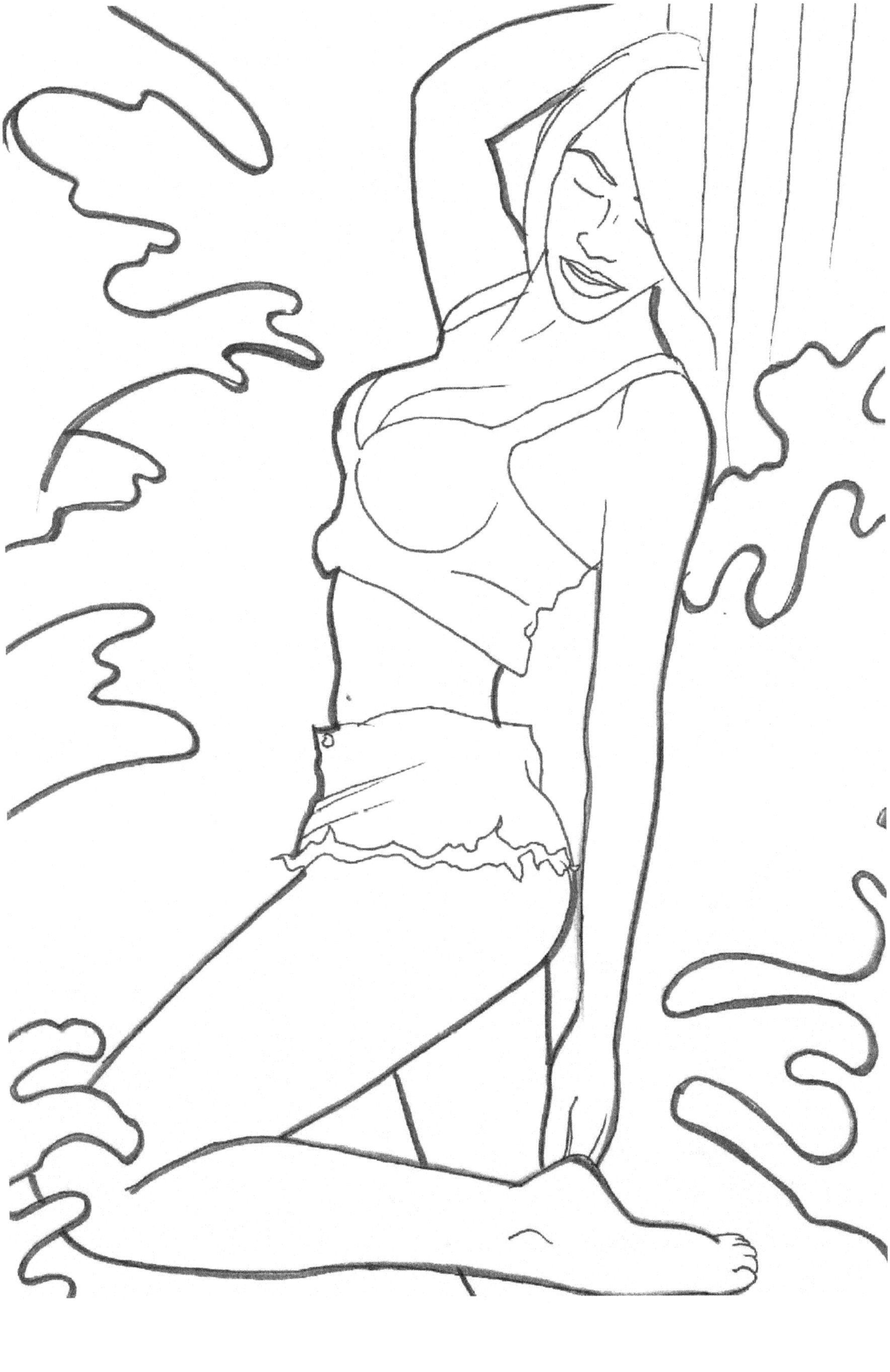

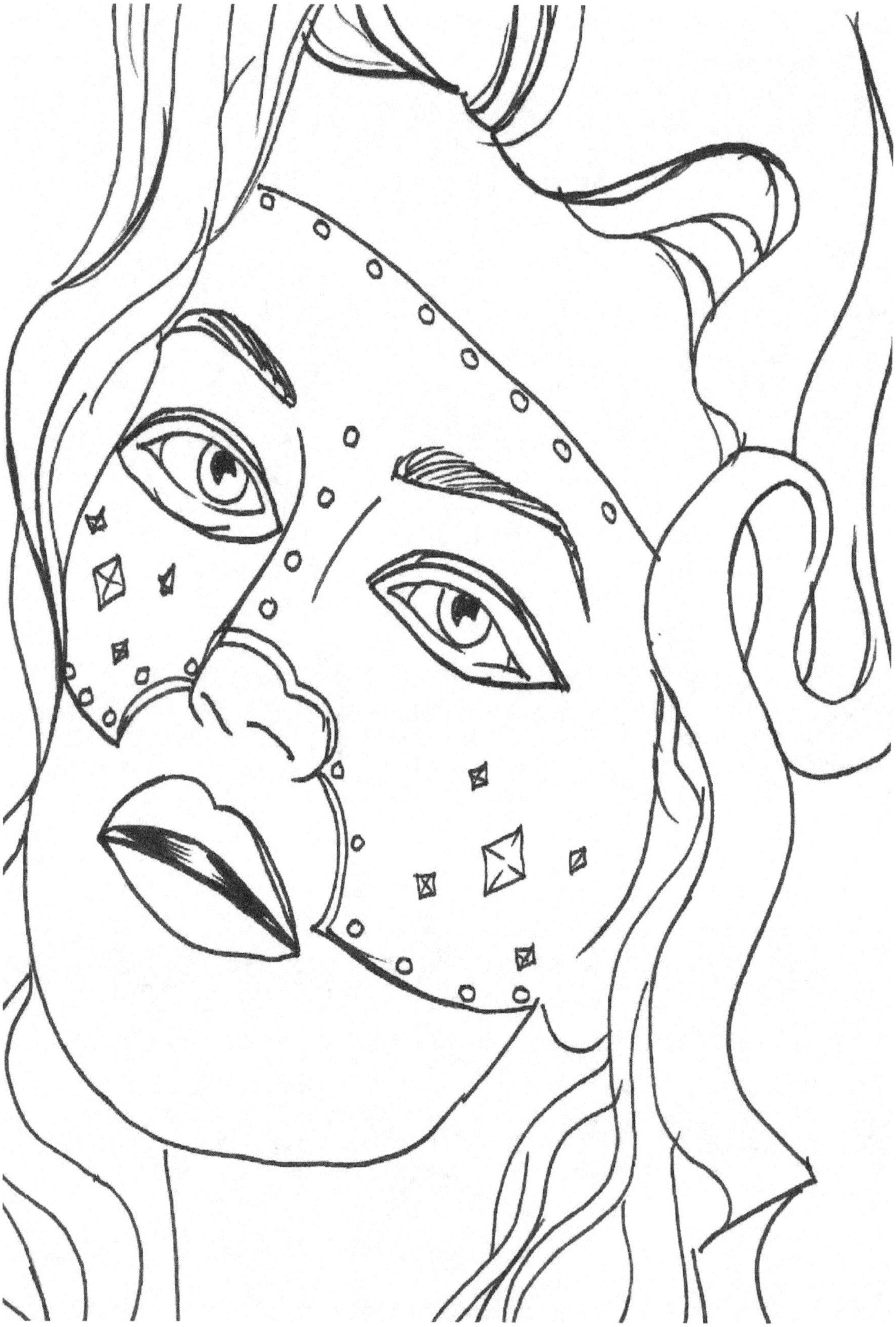

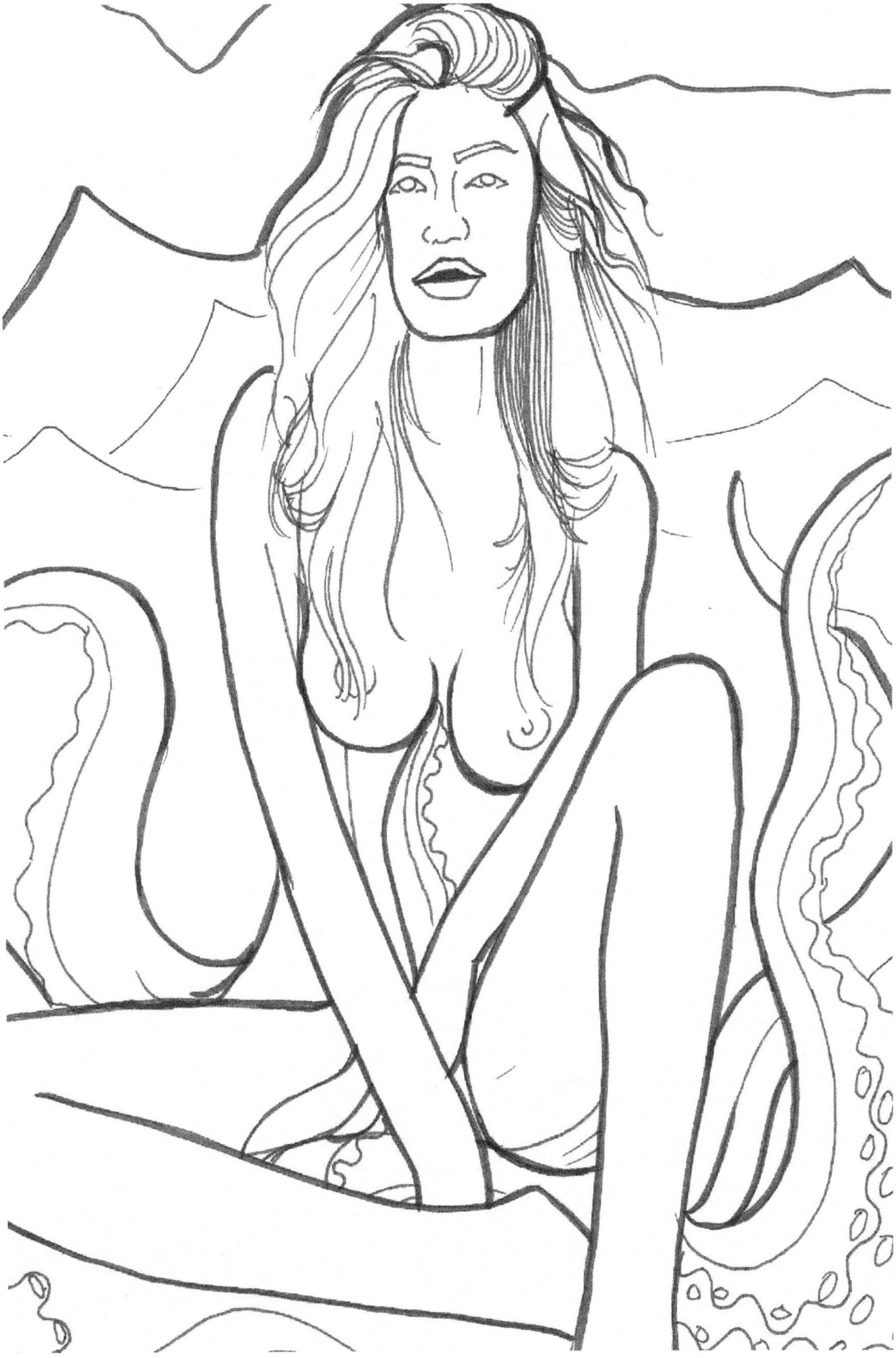

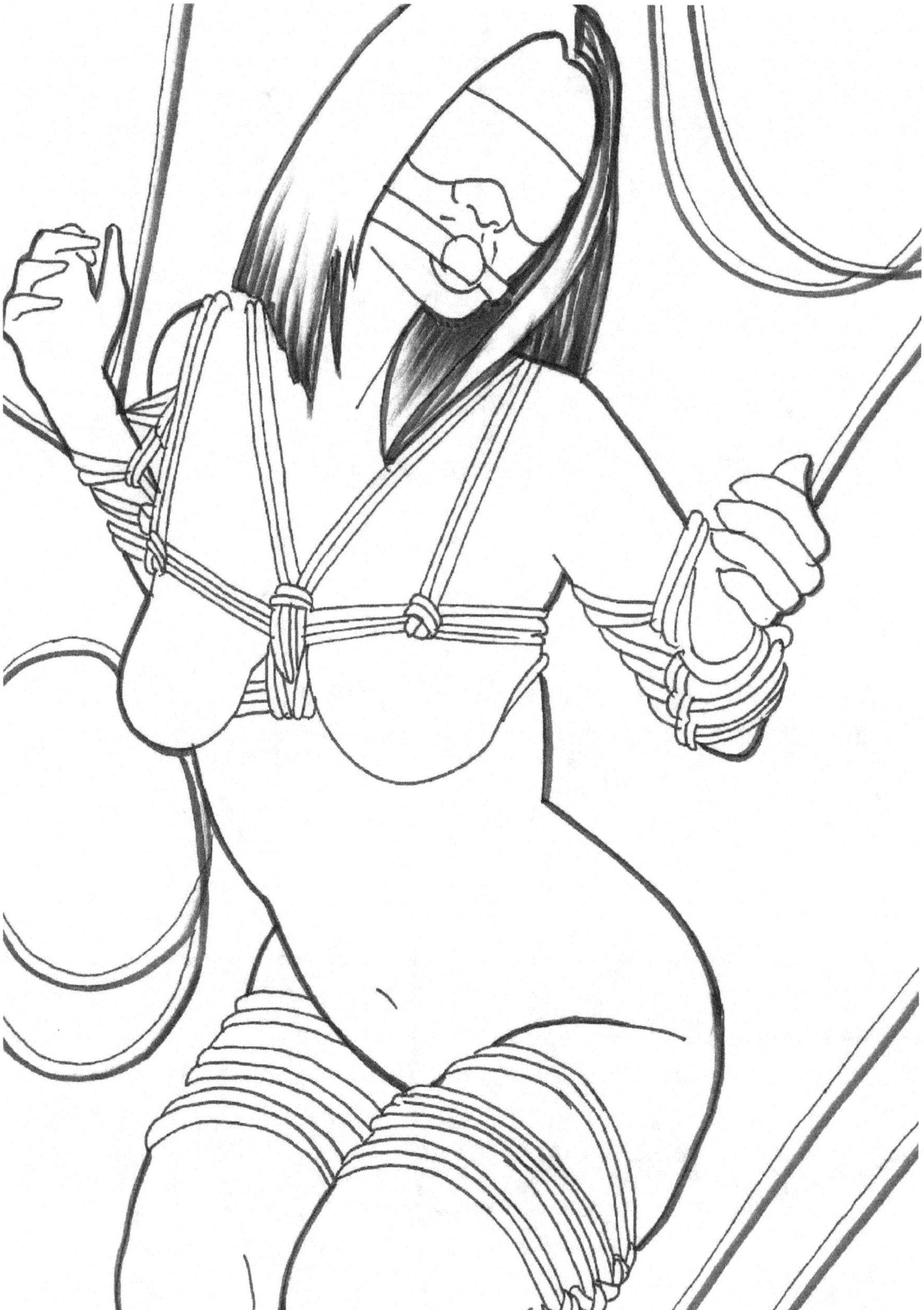

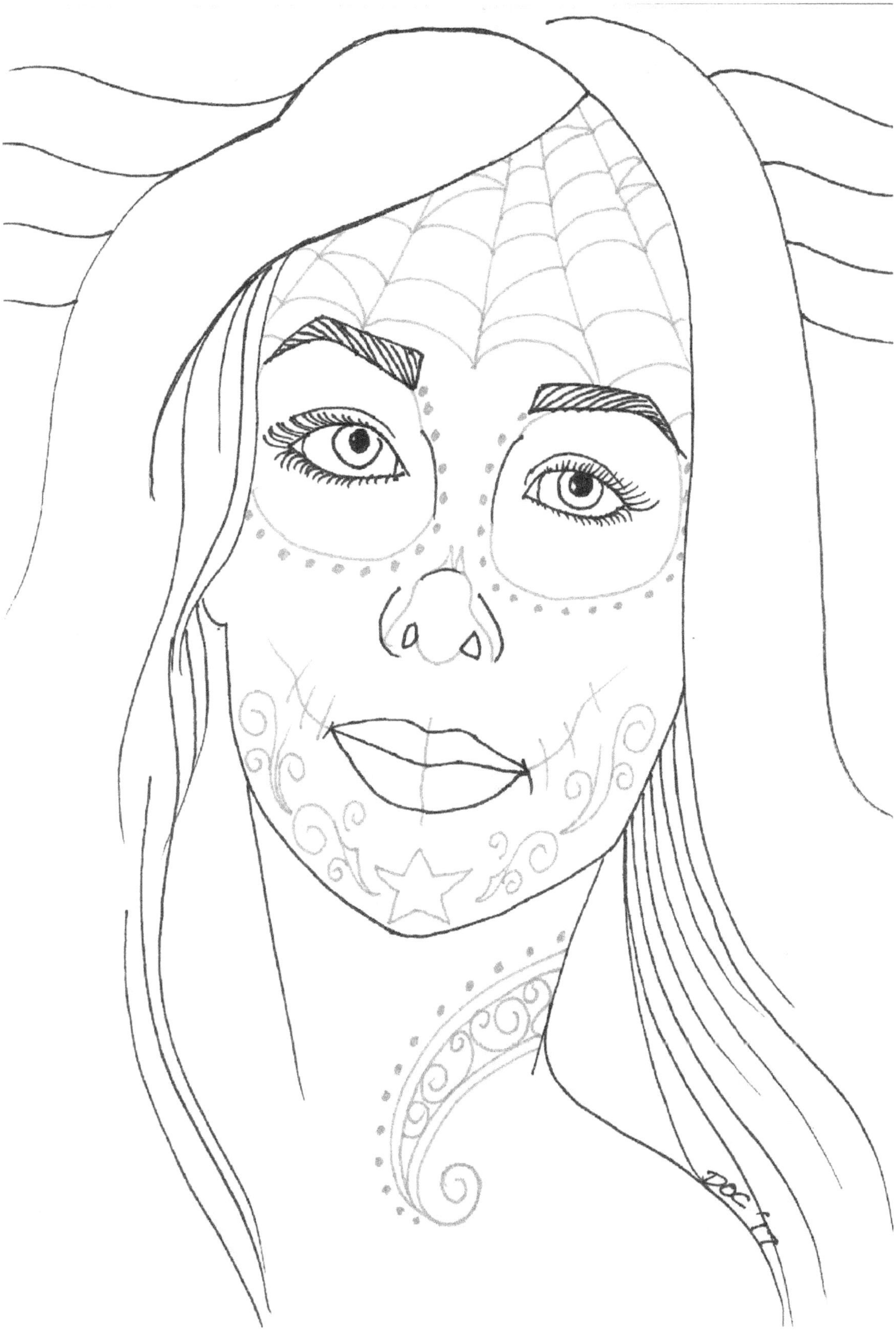

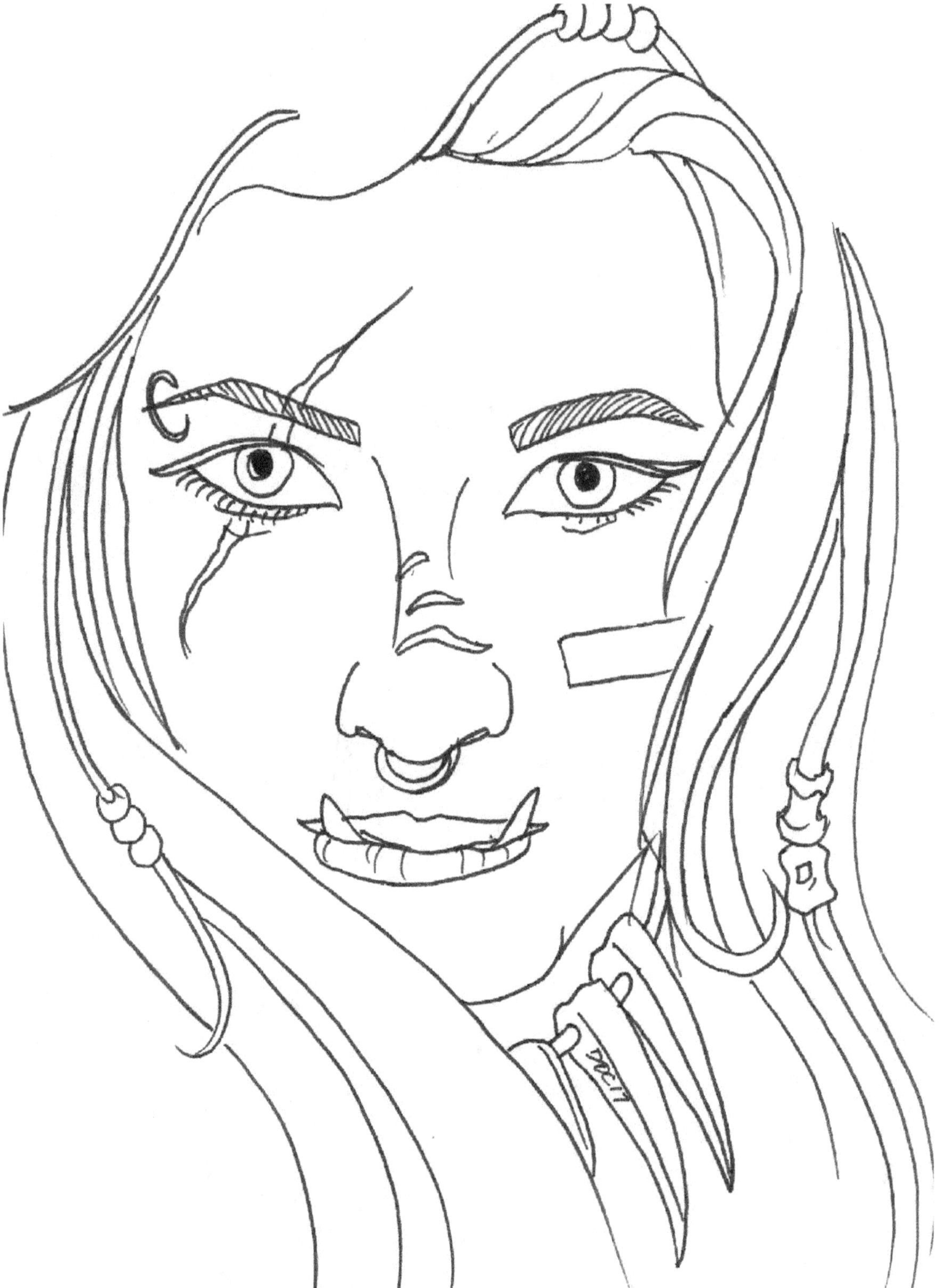

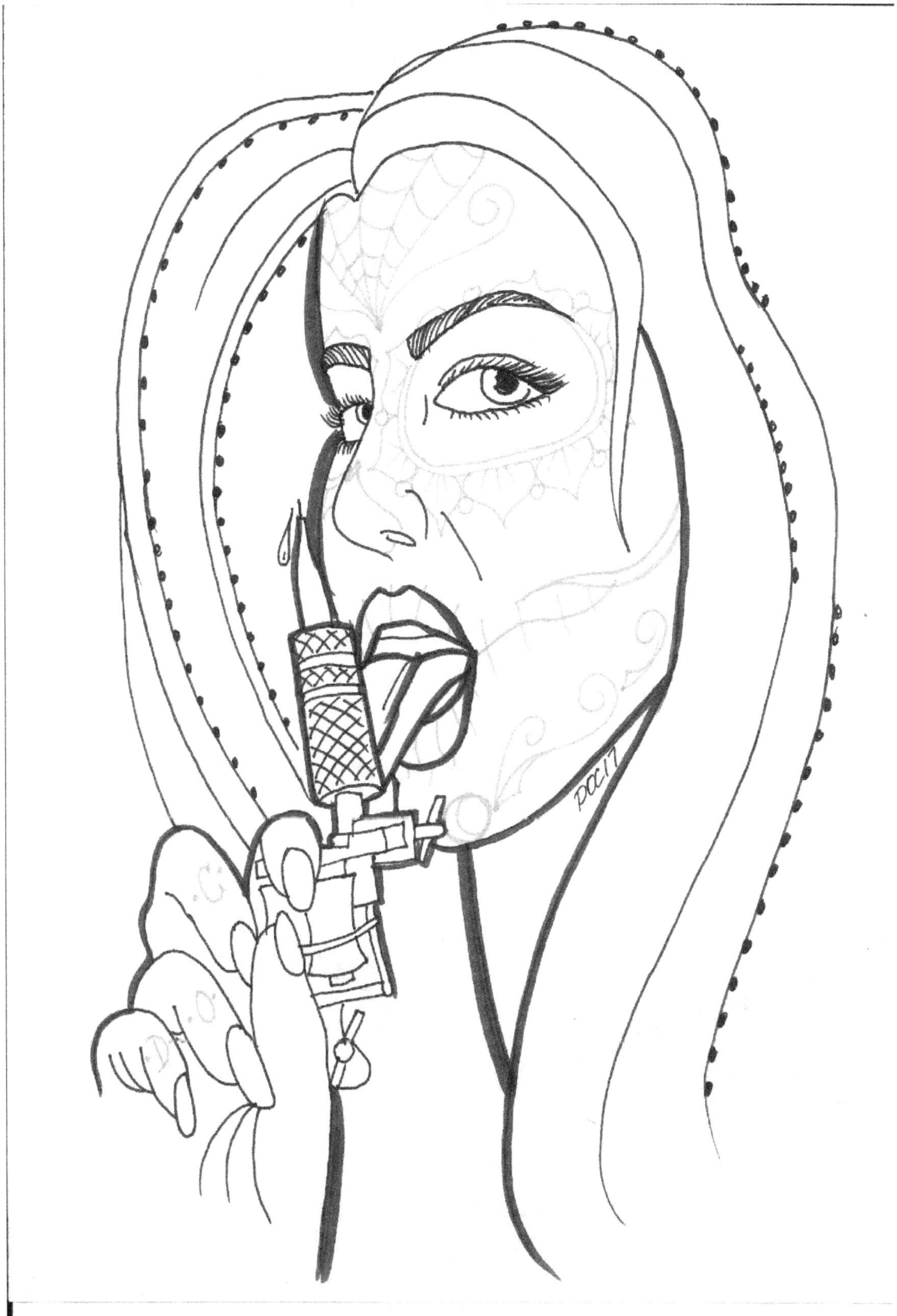
DOC17

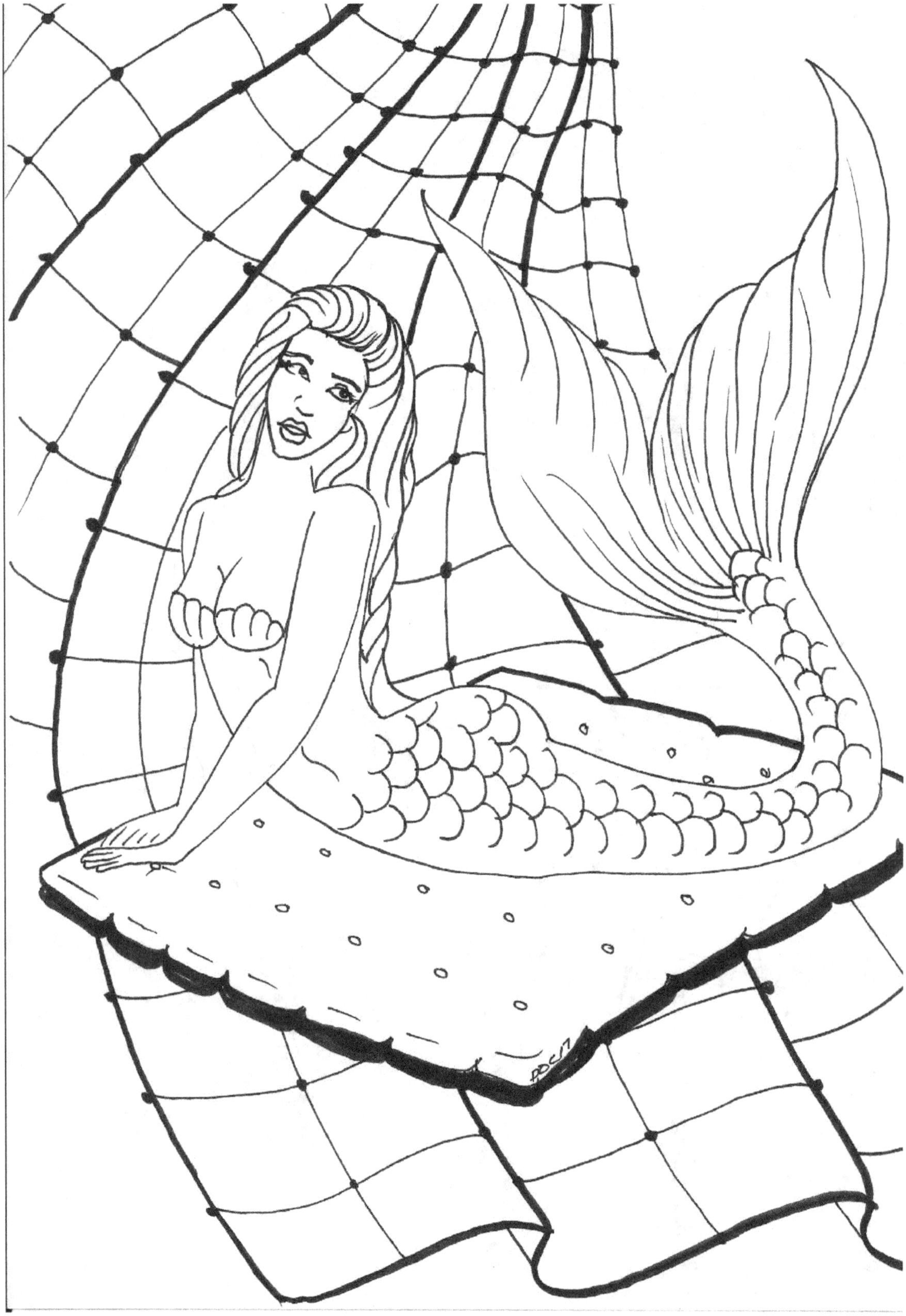

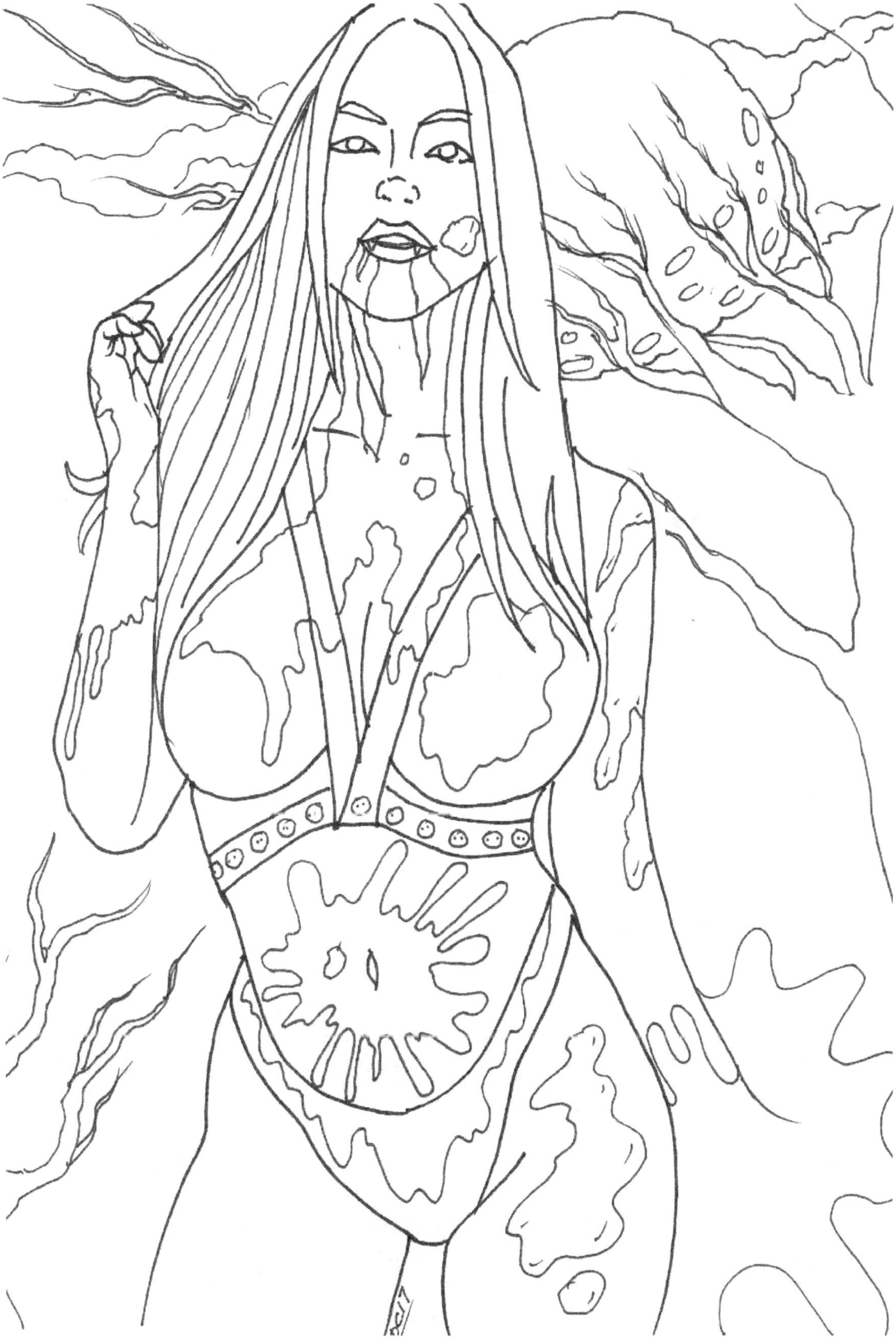

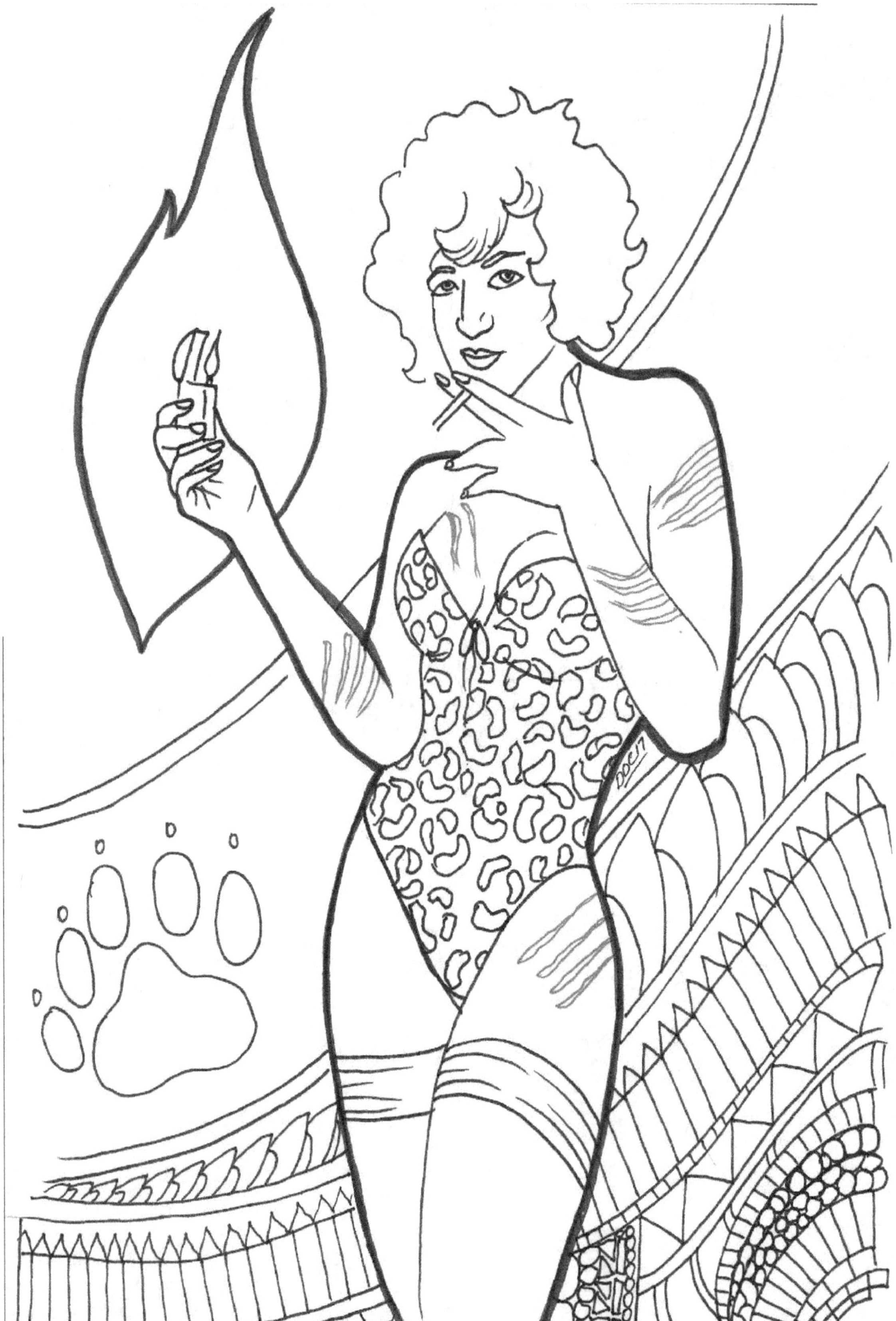

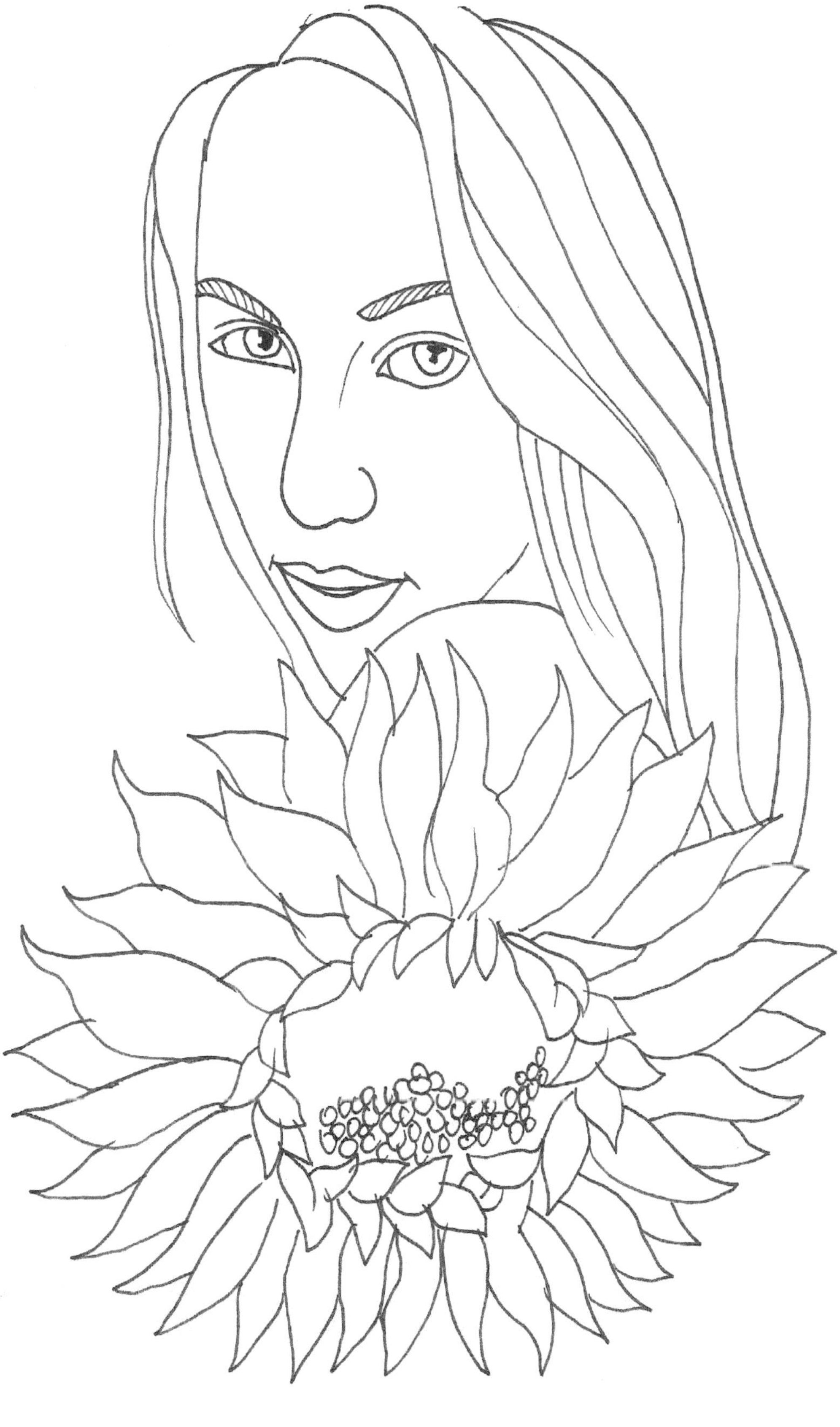

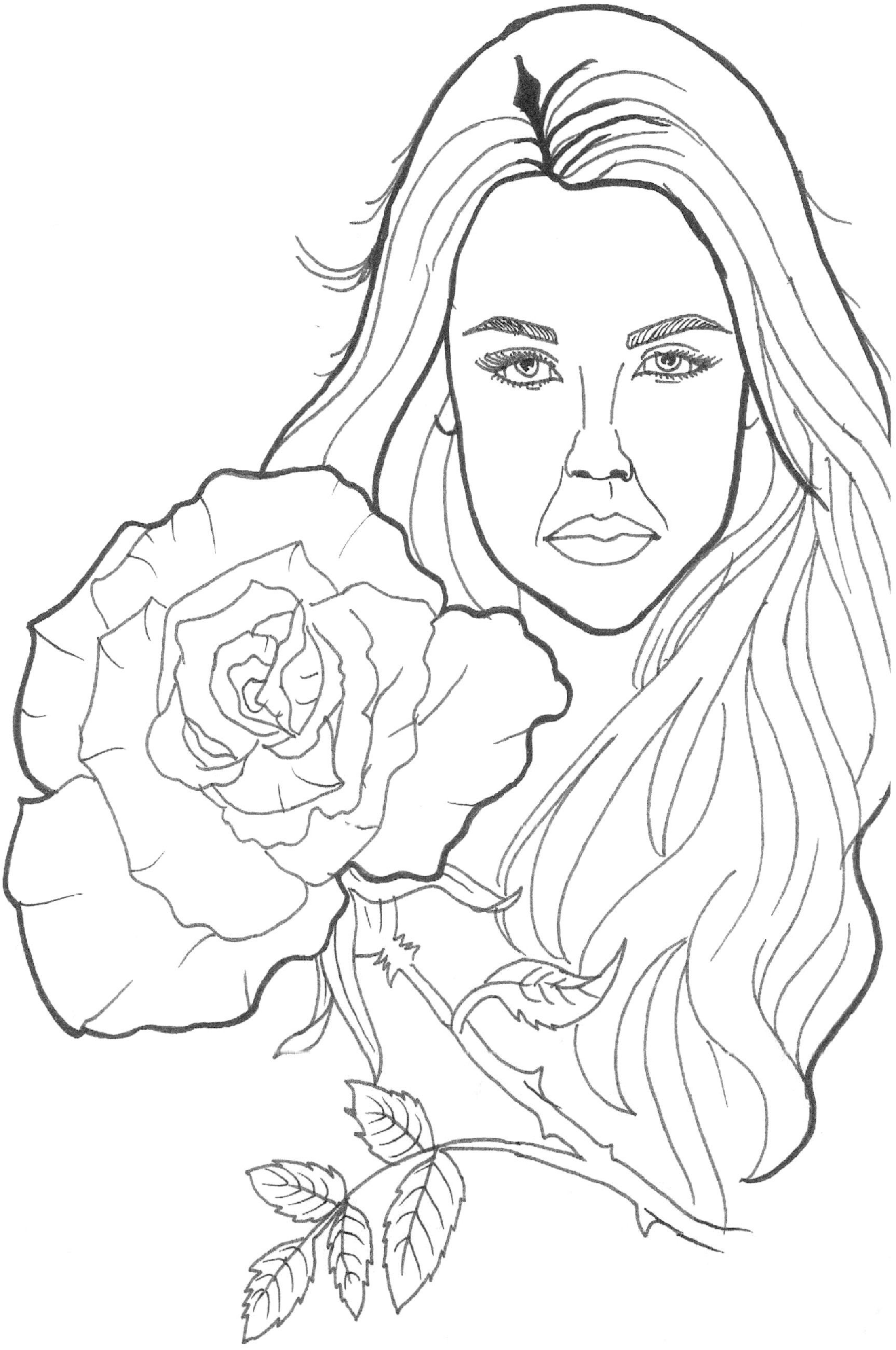

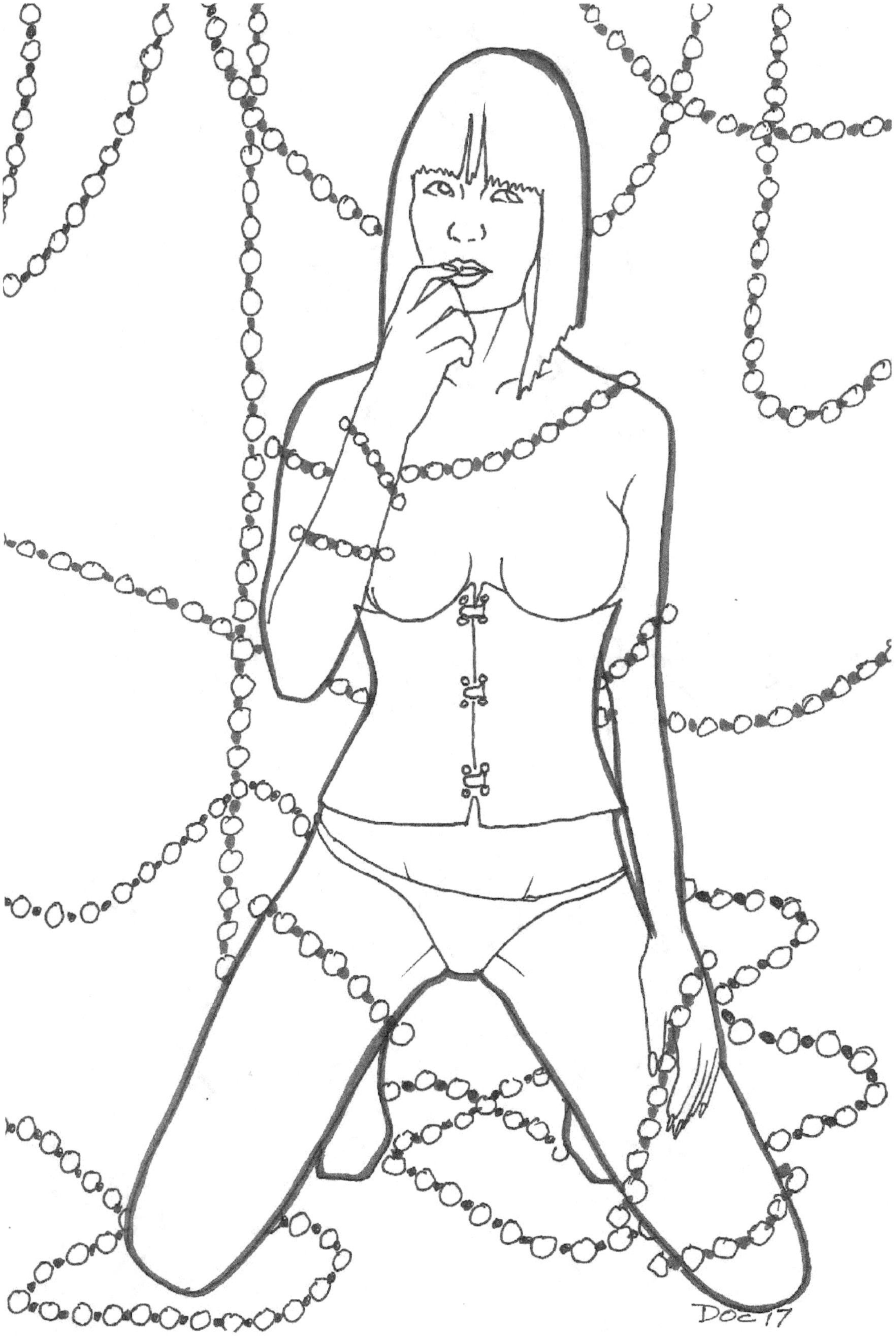
DOC 17

www.ingramcontent.com/pod-product-compliance
Lightning Source LLC
Chambersburg PA
CBHW080843170526
45158CB00009B/2619
9781365723551